Good Governance in Asia

The international aid community has advocated governance reforms as a necessary complement to economic aid to developing countries. The resultant Good Governance Agenda has been criticised for its ahistorical bias. The empirical case studies reported in this book further illustrate the limitations by showing the complex logics of governance reforms and their relations with development in the Asian context. The analysis highlights the importance of taking full notice of the Asian reform experiences in the ongoing reflection over the global institutional and development agenda. The message is not to deny the need for governance reforms, or the utility of international learning and sharing of experiences. Global development will benefit, however, from a better understanding of the linkages between governance reforms and the diverse historical conditions they are embedded in, both in developing and advanced economies.

This book was originally published as a special issue of *Journal of Contemporary Asia*.

Linda Chelan Li's work stresses the necessity to examine both dimensions of collaboration and conflict in understanding public policy and political processes. Topics she studies include the dynamics of institutional and agency change processes in central-local relations in China, government reforms, rural public finance, and education and fiscal policy.

Good Governance in Asia

Multiple Trajectories to Development

Edited by
Linda Chelan Li

Routledge
Taylor & Francis Group

LONDON AND NEW YORK

First published 2015 by Routledge

2 Park Square, Milton Park, Abingdon, Oxon, OX14 4RN
605 Third Avenue, New York, NY 10017

Routledge is an imprint of the Taylor & Francis Group, an informa business

First issued in paperback 2020

British Library Cataloguing in Publication Data
A catalogue record for this book is available from the British Library

ISBN: 978-1-138-83251-0 (hbk)
ISBN: 978-0-367-73898-3 (pbk)

Typeset in Times New Roman
by RefineCatch Limited, Bungay, Suffolk

Publisher's Note
The publisher accepts responsibility for any inconsistencies that may have arisen during the conversion of this book from journal articles to book chapters, namely the possible inclusion of journal terminology.

Disclaimer
Every effort has been made to contact copyright holders for their permission to reprint material in this book. The publishers would be grateful to hear from any copyright holder who is not here acknowledged and will undertake to rectify any errors or omissions in future editions of this book.

Contents

Citation Information

The chapters in this book were originally published in the *Journal of Contemporary Asia*, volume 44, issue 2 (May 2014). When citing this material, please use the original page numbering for each article, as follows:

Chapter 1
Multiple Trajectories and "Good Governance" in Asia: An Introduction
Linda Chelan Li
Journal of Contemporary Asia, volume 44, issue 2 (May 2014) pp. 187–203

Chapter 2
Governance Reforms in China and Vietnam: Marketisation, Leapfrogging and Retro-Fitting
Martin Painter
Journal of Contemporary Asia, volume 44, issue 2 (May 2014) pp. 204–220

Chapter 3
The Heterodoxy of Governance under Decentralisation: Rent-Seeking Politics in China's Tobacco Growing Areas
Yi-Wen Cheng & Tak-Wing Ngo
Journal of Contemporary Asia, volume 44, issue 2 (May 2014) pp. 221–240

Chapter 4
Good Governance for Environmental Protection in China: Instrumentation, Strategic Interactions and Unintended Consequences
Thomas Johnson
Journal of Contemporary Asia, volume 44, issue 2 (May 2014) pp. 241–258

Chapter 5
Governance, Courts and Politics in Asia
Björn Dressel
Journal of Contemporary Asia, volume 44, issue 2 (May 2014) pp. 259–278

Chapter 6
Pursuing Equity in Education: Conflicting Views and Shifting Strategies
Linda Chelan Li & Wen Wang
Journal of Contemporary Asia, volume 44, issue 2 (May 2014) pp. 279–297

Please direct any queries you may have about the citations to
clsuk.permissions@cengage.com

Notes on Contributors

Linda Chelan Li is Professor at the Department of Public Policy, City University of Hong Kong, China.

Yi-Wen Cheng is a Phd student at the Leiden Institute of Area Studies, Leiden University, Leiden, The Netherlands.

Björn Dressel is Senior Lecturer at the Crawford School of Public Policy, Australian National University, Australia.

Thomas Johnson is Assistant Professor at the Department of Public Policy, City University of Hong Kong, China.

Tak-Wing Ngo is Professor of Political Science at the Department of Government and Public Administration, University of Macau, China.

Martin Painter is Chair Professor Emeritus at the Department of Public Policy, City University of Hong Kong, China.

Wen Wang is Assistant Professor at the School of Public and Environmental Affairs, Indiana University-Purdue University Indianapolis, USA.

Multiple Trajectories and "Good Governance" in Asia: An Introduction

LINDA CHELAN LI

Department of Public Policy, City University of Hong Kong

ABSTRACT   *Conventional wisdom in the international aid community has been that governance systems and practices in developing countries require reform in order for aid catering to economic development or poverty alleviation to be successful. Despite criticisms, the good governance agenda has remained unscathed in international development policy until the recent economic crisis in the advanced economies. This feature section of this issue provides in-depth analysis of the nuances at the critical linkage between institutional reforms and development, based on empirical case studies of the logic of governance reforms in the Asian context. This introductory essay surveys the intellectual background of discussion over the concepts of governance, good governance and development, and the linkage between governance reforms as process and development as outcome. It highlights the significance of discussing Asian reform experiences for the ongoing reflection over the global institutional agenda. The message is not that we do not need governance reforms, or that international learning is impossible or counterproductive. Reform efforts in developing and advanced economies will benefit, however, from a better understanding of the linkage between reforms and the diverse historical conditions they are embedded in.*

Conventional wisdom in the international aid community has been that governance systems and practices in developing countries require reform in order for aid catering to economic development or poverty alleviation to be successful. The resultant good governance agenda was geared initially to sub-Saharan African countries in the late 1980s and 1990s, and later extended to countries in Asia and Latin America receiving international aid.[1] This approach makes two basic, often implicit, assumptions in what Doornbos (1995) describes as "state formation" or "reformation" processes. First, that it is theoretically possible and practically feasible to have external players initiate and influence the course of state reformation in societies suffering "bad governance." Second, an identifiable set of "good governance" institutions is available for adoption. Adding to the assumed linkage between governance and development, the resultant position becomes as follows: with successful engineering of a more or less known "template" of reforms, monitored and assisted by the international donors, an "enabling environment" can be created in the recipient societies to lay the groundwork for sustained economic growth and social well-being (Gibbon 1993; Stokke 1995a). Drawing upon experiences in Asia, this feature section seeks to challenge some of the assumptions of this position. Specifically, we shall focus on the complex interactions between the historical and institutional contexts of a society, governance reforms and development outcome through a number of in-depth case studies in the Asian context. The overall message is that there is no one single template of "good governance" institutions leading to development, and that this is a logical consequence of the heterogeneous historical landscape across societies, which demands differential developmental objectives and diverse institutional designs.

Indeed there has been a steady stream of critical reviews from various perspectives on the agenda of good governance since its inception (see, for example, Sørensen 1993; Demmers, Fernández Jilberto, and Hogenboom 2004; Rodan, Hewison, and Robison 2006). Nevertheless, institutional and capacity building programmes have become a regular feature in international lending agreements with developing countries, which by mid-2012 stood at over US$280 billion between the World Bank and the International Monetary Fund (IMF) alone.[2] Recently, the institutional emphasis received a boost when international lenders looked for a strategy to respond to the unwinding economic crises first in America and then in Europe, which were trapping an increasing number of the advanced economies. In May 2012, an Institute of Capacity Development was established within IMF after merging the former IMF Institute and its Office of Technical Assistance to gear up institutional and capacity building efforts in the advanced economies during the Eurozone economic crisis (IMF 2012). The explicit faith in the role of institutions, as shown in the following remarks of the Director of the Institute of Capacity Development, spells strong continuity in the emphasis on fostering good governance institutions so as to enable development.

> …without sound institutions, it's very hard to achieve sustainable economic growth…The current crisis in the Eurozone also highlights the importance of coherent economic and political institutions at all levels of economic development. Weaknesses in national macroeconomic and statistical institutions in supposedly "advanced" countries were at the root of the crisis, especially in Greece. And the lack of supportive fiscal and regulatory institutions at the European level – which require making additional steps in political integration – is behind the markets' continued anxiety surrounding the common European currency. The IMF takes institutions seriously. The lessons we draw from the experience of transition and the current crisis is that we neglect them at our peril (Coorey 2012).

Corollary to this emphasis on institutions is an unusual admission within the IMF that its knowledge on institutions is limited: it is not clear *which* institutions can be of help at times of economic crisis, not to mention *how* to put a desirable institution to work. In an internal, soul-searching conference, IMF Research Director Olivier Blanchard had these comments,[3]

> …we may have many policy instruments; but we are not sure how to use them…[For instance, we know that both] the relative roles of regulation and self-regulation is needed, but how we [should] combine them is extremely unclear (Blanchard 2011).

Amongst the nine "tentative conclusions" Blanchard drew for the future of macroeconomic policy in the context of the Eurozone economic crisis, there is this one:

> …Things are harder on the policy front. *Given we don't quite know how to use the new tools and they can be misused*, how should policymakers proceed? While we

have a good sense of where we want to get to, a step-by-step approach is the way to do it...Pragmatism is of the essence. This is a general theme that came up...[in] the adaptive Chinese growth model. We have to try things carefully and see how they work (Blanchard 2011, emphasis added).

It is apparent that the economic crisis in advanced Western economies has triggered a reflection amongst the rule-setters in the major international lending organisations on what was previously taken as the starting point. What is interesting is not the novelty of the questions raised, because they are not new – similar and indeed more penetrating queries have been advanced by critics of the good governance agenda geared to the developing economies for the past two decades – but that they are now surging to the forefront of considerations *within* the IMF leadership in the search for a strategy to address the fallout of economic crisis in the advanced economies.[4] The question that arises is: why is there still the emphasis on institutions given the uncertainties of their use? Has the new-found scepticism amongst IMF advisers reduced the official position on institutional capacity building to little more than rhetoric? How may we interpret and explain the rhetoric?

Intriguing as these questions are regarding the politics and sociology of IMF operations,[5] accounting for them is not the objective of the collection of papers here. The questions have, for the purpose of this feature section, vindicated at least some of the criticisms of the good governance agenda in existing literature, and the neoclassical technocratic view of development that underlines it, which the international lending organisations and governments of the donor countries in the West have persistently ignored. These papers centre on the issues of *which* specific institutions are really pertinent in relation to economic development and, even more importantly, *how* the institutions may be successfully introduced to work to the desired effect. Also of interest in Blanchard's remarks above is the favourable reference to the pragmatic approach to growth in the so-called Chinese Growth Model. The Chinese development experience has previously been categorised with other "newly industrialised economies," which is the subject of a rich literature on the "developmental state" (Johnson 1995; Evans 1995; Woo-Cumings 1999; Xia 1997). The developmental state thesis is, however, largely shunned by mainstream economic theorists, who attributed the remarkable economic growth in these economies since the 1960s and their apparently different development trajectory to the unique cultural and historical characteristics of those societies. This effectively minimises the threat of these alternative development experiences to the governance reform and macro structural adjustment agendas which the World Bank and IMF peruse across the board.

This feature section presses the case that the complex linkage between history, institutions and development requires further attention. Drawing on in-depth case studies of governance reform experiences in Asia, each of the five contributions dwells on a specific dimension in this linkage and special attention is paid to actors and their agency. In addition to the "what" and "how" questions asked in most analyses, a greater focus on actors and their role in shaping the "logics" of reform directs us to revisit the often forgotten "why" question. Why are the "right" institutions not introduced earlier? What accounts for the difficulties and obstacles to their adoption in developing economies? Here we blend the focus on interests and power relations in social conflict theory and the insights on the role of the historical and institutional contexts of the historical institutionalists. Before we preview the gist of the discussion and contribution of the papers, let us first define what we mean by governance, good governance and development in the context of discussions in the literature, as well as the linkage between good governance institutional reforms and development.

Governance and Good Governance

The first major, and obvious, question in a discussion of good governance reforms is what "governance" and "good governance" mean. Despite its popularity the concept of "governance" is highly ambiguous and excessively broad, and has remained so today notwithstanding numerous attempts to clarify it. Indeed the elasticity of the concept is suggested as the key to its attraction, as Doornbos (2001, 95) traces the intellectual context of the emergence of "governance" in academic and policy discourse:

> the notion of "governance" had an *a priori* attractiveness…as it could refer to complexities entailing a good deal more than [sound] administration or management, namely the element of political restructuring and the handling of this, while at the same time including the administrative-management dimension…(I)t opened the window for a focus on how "politics" or the political process was conducted and embedded within larger structures.

The concept introduces the political dimension into an otherwise technocratic discourse of public issues but in such a way that allows more flexibility than an explicitly political approach. In practice, it enables the user to maintain a camouflage of political neutrality when necessary as governance discussions span the vast space between the political-technical continuum and may hence be adjusted more towards one end or the other as circumstances require. The expansiveness of the concept goes further as governance literally can mean many different things to different people. One attempt summarises the diverse meanings in the dimensions of substantive content and character (Hyden, Court, and Mease 2004, 12). Along the first are those who define governance as basically the *rules* of conducting public business on one end, and those who see governance as the activities of *steering* public affairs on the other. The second dimension contrasts those who emphasise governance as *process*, and those who see governance as *results or outcomes* of public decision-making. Each of the various meanings – rules, steering, process or outcome – consists of highly variable contents. For example, in their preferred definition of governance as "a meta-activity that influences outcomes," Hyden, Court, and Mease (2004, 16) focus on rules and processes *vis-à-vis* activities and outcomes. It is however unclear *what* exactly is involved in the meta-activity of rule formation, apart from the formal and informal rules which feature prominently as intervening outputs. There should be, apparently, requirements of the style and character of the formation process of the rules, and even the substantive contents of the rules, but these remain undefined and are thus left to the imagination of the reader.

Governance is, by and large, taken as synonymous with "development policy management" in the discourse of international development assistance and as such denotes a kind of "steering activity" and has a strong administrative and managerial character (Gibbon 1993; Leftwich 1993; World Bank 1992, 1). When the adjective "good" was added to it, and the good governance agenda as a normative project emerged in the international aid regime in the aftermath of the World Bank 1989 Report on *Sustainable Growth*, the scope of conditions attached to development aid substantially extended from macro-economic balances in the Structural Adjustment Programmes (SAP) of the 1980s to a whole range of socio-political institutions encompassing anti-poverty, greater transparency and democratisation. By the late 1980s it was apparent that the earlier SAPs put in place in African countries had failed, and there was pressure for a response. The dominant mood amongst the lenders was that SAPs had failed not because of problems with the SAPs *per se*, but because the institutional infrastructure in the host countries was often too weak to enable their effective execution (Stein and Nafziger 1991; Gibbon 1993). A "crisis in governance" underlined the crisis in economic development in Africa, it was argued (World Bank 1989). A subtle shift of paradigm has taken place, from a "less state, more market" formula towards a more political-institutionalist approach calling for a "better state" (Demmers, Fernández Jilberto, and Hogenboom 2004, 2). The good governance agenda would thus, through the grooming of appropriate institutions, foster an enabling environment and governance infrastructure in the aid-recipient countries to facilitate development.

The question is: which institutions will constitute an enabling environment for development in the developing economies? As it turns out, the template has largely adopted the clusters of Western governance institutions: an independent judiciary and rule of law, fiscal accountability and independent auditing, a representative legislature, respect for human rights, a pluralistic civil society and freedom of the press, and so on (World Bank 1989; Leftwich 1993, 610). This dominance of Western-conceived institutions as part of the political conditionality of international lending arrangements has been criticised as symbolising imperialism (Demmers, Fernández Jilberto, and Hogenboom 2004, 7). Despite the obvious emphasis on the political, a heavy technocratic screen has been employed to downplay its political character, and to represent the institutional efforts as essentially a matter of straightforward application of science.[6] It has been said that international lenders, even more than academic analysts, have a need for a concept whose meaning is sufficiently flexible to serve their varied organisational purposes: "The attractiveness of the concept of Good Governance lies in its capacity to make complex issues seem manageable, to hide disagreement and to provide a practical answer to the disappointing results of the Structural Adjustment Programmes of the 1980s" (Demmers, Fernández Jilberto, and Hogenboom 2004, 2).

The critique on aid imperialism finds support in the work of the historical institutionalists, who have questioned the empirical rationale of the good governance template, pointing out that many of the institutions that developing countries are required to adopt as part of the loan agreements were *not* present at the time of economic growth and development in today's advanced economies, but were only introduced *afterwards* (Goldsmith 2007). There is also no clear boundary of this essentially political conditionality (Sørensen 1993; Stokke 1995b), as the list of institutions contained in the package keeps expanding. In one count, the number of good governance "aspects" to be promoted through institutional reforms and capacity building programmes as reported in successive World Development Reports of the World Bank more than doubles from 45 in 1997 to 116 in 2002 (Grindle 2004, 527).

Development

Development is the *raison d'être* of all the discussions and efforts over governance and good governance, and not surprisingly the ambivalence of meanings in the latter has been mirrored in definitions of development. Indeed, while the common-sense meaning of the concept may appear self-evident and straightforward, as denoting an improvement to the pre-existing situation for "betterment" of well-being or welfare, clarity fades as soon as more specificity is sought. Values and politics permeate the definition of "improvement," the identification of constituent dimensions of "well-being" and the relative weights of each, as well as the choice of priority intervention. Development is essentially "a moving target," varying across time and space (Hyden, Court, and Mease 2004, 7).[7]

Sometimes clarity suffers from the way the literature addresses the concept: development as objective and outcome is often conflated with the approaches to development (Demmers, Fernández Jilberto, and Hogenboom 2004, 2–3). In this collection we see development as both objective and outcome, *notwithstanding* its close links with approaches to development. What defines development has been variable and a mixed bag, where the contents have changed and kept on changing over the years.[8]

Amongst the various definitions is the one which sees development as, essentially, economic growth. Rooted in the neoclassical theory, this view of development was especially dominant during the 1950s, and still remains today the ultimate concern behind development policy (Leftwich 2000, 40–44). Closely related to this view is the modernisation theory, which sees development of all societies making the transition from "the traditional" towards "the modern" (Törnquist 1999). The approach to development is, accordingly, to supply additional resources of capital and skills to help the recipient economies remain "on track" in modernising. The specific socio-economic-political contexts of the host societies receiving aid are regarded as of minimal relevance to this process and to the impact of development assistance. Since all societies are assumed to undergo a similar trajectory towards modernity, the experiences of the more developed West are, by simple logic, directly relevant to the late-comers. Development assistance, in this view, becomes a non-political and straightforward process of resource provision and know-how transfer. Development policy management – a synonym for governance in international aid circles – is reduced, by and large, to a matter of good management and coordination of this resource allocation process within and between the donor and the aid recipient.

Such a view of development as economic growth and the corresponding technocratic and managerial approach to it was gradually seen to be inadequate. Beginning from the 1960s, failures of previous development programmes made it clear that recipient societies required assistance of a broader sort, and that the historical contexts and different baselines of various host societies had greater significance than earlier anticipated. Developing economy governments were often weak and lacked the technical capacity and incentives to achieve sustained economic growth. There was also a substantial gap between growth rates and the general well-being of the people at large, given distributional issues. Increasingly, there was recognition that development needed to be social as well as economic, and should encompass explicitly the substantive socio-economic values of poverty alleviation and a more equitable wealth distribution. Development assistance policy accordingly adjusted, and anti-poverty and structural adjustment measures emerged (World Bank 1981; Leftwich 2000, 42, 109). Conspicuously marking this broadening of the development agenda is the establishment of United Nations institutions, such as the United Nations Research Institute for Social Development (set up in 1963) and United Nations Development Programme (which commenced work in 1965).

Then there was politics. Emerging in the same way as the socio-economic interpretation above, a more political interpretation of development – and in this case a certain direction of development, namely towards democratisation, is a result of the failures of the pre-existing notions and development policy measures (Leftwich 1993). As noted previously, towards the end of the 1980s, the failure of adjustment programmes gave rise to the call for aid initiatives directed at the governance infrastructure of the host countries. The optimism for change was, then, encouraged by the end of the Cold War which on the one hand lent greater legitimacy to the globalisation of the Western-based institutions amongst the recipient countries whilst on the other required the Western governments, in the absence of security concerns, to justify to their electorates the continuation of aid to authoritarian governments.

The importance of the political in the concept of development, and in the approach to development, is especially emphasised by the social conflict theorists. Development is essentially political, to be explained as a function of the deep-rooted power relations in society over time (Rodan, Hewison, and Robison 2006; Leftwich 2000). What is required are questions of "why" rather than "how." The former turns the analyst to issues of interest and power, the latter, matters of skills, timing, and contingency. The social conflict critics are also critical to the "institutional turn" of the international aid regime character-ising the good governance agenda, lamenting that the emphasis on the role of the state leaves intact the neoliberal bias for a specific form of capitalistic development. In other words, while politics, and the state, is said to have a large role in development, only a *certain type* of state – namely, neoliberal – has been considered conducive to a preferred genre of capitalist development.[9] The broadening of the concept of development to include poverty alleviation and democratisation has not materially affected the dominance of the traditional technocratic stress premising efficiency and procedural propriety, with the socio-political approaches assuming largely a peripheral significance (Demmers, Fernández Jilberto, and Hogenboom 2004; Doornbos 2001, 95). The deep political questions of power relations that underline the difficulties of development in developing countries have continued to be swept aside in the governance reforms (Rodan, Hewison, and Robison 2006, 4). Indeed, structural adjustment programmes have been re-introduced alongside the new good governance initiatives, buttressing the view that the governance approach is to complement adjustment programmes to enable the idealised market to work *better*; it is not an alternative to a failed, superseded course (Stein and Nafziger 1991).

Critical Linkage? Roles of and Limits to Institutions

Given the predispositions of the various formulations of "governance" and "develop-ment," this feature issue takes governance largely in its "process sense," aiming at bringing about development as an outcome. Governance is sometimes also used in an output sense as governance practices that the institutional reform process is to bring about, like the rule of law, greater respect of transparency and accountability in government affairs, or an independent judiciary. Whilst it is where the boundaries between governance and development start to blur, as outputs and outcomes are by nature analytical distinc-tions, their process-outcome relationship has posed the most critical questions. Do governance institutions really affect development? Which institutions matter, or matter more? Can institutions be "put in place" from the outside?

Some of these questions have been addressed above. Here we shall focus on two issues. First is the susceptibility of institutions to deliberate efforts of "engineering." Second is the practical feasibility of the good governance agenda being pursued by the international community in their development aid programmes. Towards the first, more fundamental, challenge institutionalists have cast doubt on whether, and how, institutions could play an *independent* role in economic growth and political development (Engerman and Sokoloff 2008; Acemoglu, Johnson, and Robinson 2005) as it is immensely difficult to distinguish the effects of an institution from those of its conditions and environment (Przeworski 2004). Glaeser and colleagues (2004) examine the indicators commonly employed to support the argument for the role of institutions in economic growth, and conclude that most are, in fact, methodologically flawed. The ambiguous relation between institution as cause and development as effect means that any institutional reform designed with such a causation relationship assumed or anticipated stands on slippery ground. Accordingly, there is a need to temper the ambitious claim of causation. In doing so, and to reduce the degree of "slippage" between institutional design and outcome in international development programmes, careful analysis of the actual conditions of each society needs to be applied to customise reform designs (Przeworski 2004, 540).

Practically speaking, the key concern is that *even if* development was a largely managerial and technical exercise, and the appropriateness of the standard package was not an issue, adopting the long list of good governance practices as demanded by international lenders – from transparency to human rights and to balanced terms of payments – would require so much support in the wider environment in developing societies that the development program would not be sustainable. Indeed, the failure of the SAPs in the 1980s serves as a reminder as the lack of support in the host countries has been said to be at least a partial factor (Painter 2002; Stein and Nafziger 1991).

A direct response to the expansive scope of prescriptions is to narrow it. This is the argument of Grindle (2004)'s "good enough governance" thesis: if a full template is not manageable, then limit its scope by focusing efforts on the core institutions. However, the problem of this approach surfaces immediately on execution. It is abundantly vague as to how one may justifiably delineate the subset of the template which constitutes the core, or "good enough," institutions. Will the list vary across different host countries, how and why, or why not?

Matthew Andrews' (2008) empirical analysis of the institutional mixes in a selection of "good" and "not so good" governments finds that even for countries commonly recognised as well governed, their institutions vary considerably over a number of core dimensions. Moreover, often the poorly governed countries, as a group, do *not* exhibit a significant difference in these institutional dimensions from the well-governed countries. These findings suggest that the linkage between institutional forms as we know them and development and governance as outcomes is more nuanced than the linear causation assumption the good governance agenda leads us to believe. The good governance institutions are, in practice, more like "a set of items on a long menu" from which countries pick and choose than definitive guides to good governance and development as outcome (Andrews 2008, 2). The "pick and choose" processes signify the presence and the role of other factors, including variable mixes of actors and their varied agency, the historical baseline of institutional and other conditions, working through a contingency framework (Andrews 2008, 31). To some extent this comes close to Przeworski (2004)'s emphasis on heeding the "actual conditions" when designing institutions.

Comparative empirical studies have questioned the assumed causality between the emergence of good governance institutions historically and the occurrence of economic development (Goldsmith 2007; Li 2009). The mixes of institutions that induce economic development are more varied than the standard template put forward by the international aid community, as "the roads to good governance are not paved in a linear or identical fashion" (Hyden, Court, and Mease 2004, 3). Indeed, if history is of any guide, past trajectories of contemporary democracies – which all developed from non-democratic or colonial regimes – suggest that economic growth and political change could take place, and have taken place, under conditions of "bad governance." A key problem with Grindle's (2004) "good enough governance" thesis is that it still requires the identification of a core bundle of institutions. Short of a clear articulation of the yardstick of inclusion of some and exclusion of others, and an answer to the question of variability, resorting to a reduced list of "good enough" institutions amounts to rationalising *post hoc* whatever is executed in practice, which is clearly unsatisfactory.

The message drawn from these critiques is that the removal of the more egregious features of bad governance, such as large-scale corruption, gross inequities and oppressive treatment of populations, is more complex than the application of a pre-specified package of good governance institutions can deliver. Achieving economic growth and social well-being is the outcome of a long historical process in which many factors are involved. Institutions are one of those factors, and likely an important one, but their endogenous nature means that effects of institutions are inevitably intertwined with other factors, like geography and human agency (Sachs 2003). It is nearly impossible to delineate any *one* mix of institutions as guide-posts to good governance and development across different countries, as countries vary in conditions (which mean those factors other than institutions) and history (which is the summation of conditions and institutions and their cumulative effects over time). The effects of an institution on development will similarly vary across countries, nullifying any global good governance and good institution agenda.

Ruling out the "one template" model might relieve the international aid community of the impossible mission of dealing with an ever-lengthening must-do list, as well as the demanding obligation of securing the right mix and sufficient amount of resources to establish the required institutions. However, it leaves open the next step: *what* may still be done to foster good, or better, governance in developing countries, if there is no one reform agenda to prescribe and work for. Despite all the criticisms against the one-template thesis, that *some* institutions do have a certain role in fostering growth and development is shared by critics and advocates alike of the good governance agenda.[10] What sets apart the critics from the advocates is more about practical stance than cognitive conception. The critics have emphasised the intellectual fallacy of the model, whilst the advocates have stressed its practical value in the world of actions and *realpolitik*. The "good-enough" thesis seeks to rescue the good governance agenda by tempering its scope, but it stops short of satisfactorily specifying *which* institutions constitute the core subset of institutions. On the other hand, the emphasis placed by some historical institutionalists on the importance of contexts and designing institutions for different countries also has serious limits, as contextualism is almost a "truism" (King 1995). The abstract emphasis on context by historical institutionalists will not serve any meaningful purpose for developing countries badly in need of help. If a single, universal, template of governance reforms is inadequate, developing societies need manageable advice targeting their needs at their respective stages of development.

What is needed is *specific* information about the particular conditions of a country, and knowledge – or educated guesses – of how these conditions may be changed as a result of the introduction of a *certain* institution or policy. There is a need to go beyond the preponderant emphasis on abstract principles at both ends, namely the applicability of a fixed one-template model (full or abridged version) to all kinds of historical conditions across countries on the one hand, and varying institutional design in accordance with particularistic contexts on the other. Societies in need of advice, and these include the developing economies and the more advanced ones, require practical pointers regarding how to match their particular contexts and institutional designs. To meet this demand poses new challenges. For example, how should we approach the task of understanding particular historical contexts of societies? Given the varied expectations and definitions of development and varying baselines of the infrastructural base in different societies, how may we arrive at some practical suggestions on what and how to reform for the sake of better development?

All empirically based and drawn from rich case materials in Asia, the five contributions in this feature section seek to go some way in addressing these questions on linkages between governance institutional reforms, or governance as process, and governance and development as outcome. Whilst giving consideration to the conditions and histories of societies concerned, the contributions have paid explicit attention to delineating the specific logics of reform in the respective contexts, including the role of actors' interests and interactions. The historical context is "disaggregated" to identify the specific aspects of institutional arrangements (for example, the territoriality and multi-tier governance dimension, and implementation) and historical conditions (stages of market development; level of public service provision) that are contingent to events, and their roles analysed (see Painter 2014; Cheng and Ngo 2014; Johnson 2014). Unintended consequences are captured and the context whereby they take place, often as a result of actors' strategic interactions, is analysed, supplying the details of what is often glossed over as "contingency." A comparative framework, whether between Asian states (Dressel 2014) or between the two largest economies in the developing and advanced worlds (Li and Wang 2014), further brings out the impacts of differential historical and institutional conditions for governance reforms – a strong judiciary and equitable education, respectively – in advancing development in these respective societies.

Institutional Logics: No Template or Sequencing of Reform

The contributions by Painter on governance reforms in China and Vietnam, and by Cheng and Ngo on China's tobacco industry, turn on its head the neoclassical conception of good governance institutions by highlighting the diversity of reform contents and heterogeneity of development trajectories. Painter takes issue with the sequencing argument, popularised by major international donors, which assigns institutions to different stages of reform. In developing their public service infrastructure, it was said that developing countries should first introduce the rule-bound, Weberian-style bureaucracy, a first-stage type of institution, before they could safely introduce decentralised, market-mimicking models of service delivery in second-stage reforms. This advice was apparently ignored in China and Vietnam where extensive marketisation reforms of the second-stage genre unfolded when many first-stage reforms – like the development of rule of law and more participative and transparent government decision-making process – had yet to see their impacts.

In Painter's analysis, these seemingly "bad governance" policies were not accidents, nor were they outcomes of mistakes or negligence by political elites. Rather, they have followed their own logic, and many policies were deliberately taken in view of the constraints of the broader conditions (market, administrative, political) to serve important developmental objectives. Despite the original expectations of government, some of these "bad governance" policies have subsequently led to the adoption of good governance measures. Seen in a longer temporal perspective, governance reforms in these transition economies might have "leapfrogged" and "retro-fitted" as they navigated through the circumstances of the specific historical conditions with "home-grown" rationales. What Painter has come to is, however, more than a re-ordering of the desired or presumed sequence of reform as depicted in the good governance discourse. By elaborating on the reform logics based on the evolving market-plan relations in China and Vietnam, Painter shows that the definition of development objectives is context- (including time-) specific. Development is largely a normative concept and its meaning changes in varying time and space, accordingly demanding also differential institutional arrangements. As Pierson (2004) stresses a temporal dimension for politics, so Painter calls into question the assumption that only certain institutions will work for economic development. Possibilities exist for *both* alternative sequencing of a given list of institutional reforms, as well as a different list altogether, in achieving good governance and development.

It is on the conceptualisation of good governance that Cheng and Ngo (2014) begin their analysis. They argue that the stylised categorisation of good-bad governance of the neoliberal paradigm cannot capture the full complexity of accountabilities in a large political system. The impact of "state scaling" is the highlight of the argument here. Whilst most studies on governance tend to focus on the national level, treating the local dimensions of governance mostly in passing, this study dissects the webs of institutional arrangements in China at the national, regional and local levels, focusing on tobacco regulation and production, and the changes over the past 20 years. In this multi-tier web, interests are shown to be diverse, goals often contradicted, and the strategic interactions of actors at "horizontal" tiers and "vertical" systems have brought about paradoxical governance outcomes. This finding drives home the risk of a blanket application of the good governance agenda, irrespective of actual conditions: the implementation of good governance institutions (higher level of transparency and accountability) *could* lead to bad governance outcomes (peasants' welfare being impaired).

Similar to Painter, Cheng and Ngo stress the importance of the institutional environment in which the reform measures were introduced. The culprit for the paradoxical governance outcome was the multi-tiered fiscal-administrative governance framework and the way it crisscrossed with the vertical system of tobacco administration. The way revenues and expenditures were historically allocated in the state system mandated a conflict of interests between the national and local governments, as both were propelled to maximise their respective revenues to meet expenditure needs. In other words, to the extent that local government poses a *chosen* dilemma for public administrators (Stewart 1985, 24) so that the structural tension between local responsiveness and national equity can be contained but not resolved, the state-scaling institutions in China have produced contradictory incentives for the various actors involved that have served to magnify the tension. Consequently, reforms that were designed to improve the efficiency of national regulation of the tobacco industry subsequently turned against the benefits of the tobacco leaf peasants.

Like Painter, Cheng and Ngo draw attention back to the starting point of the good governance agenda: what makes some institutions "good" versus "bad" and justifies their inclusion or exclusion from the reform template? What does "good governance" ultimately mean and seek to achieve? The answer in these two papers highlights the historical embeddedness of governance institutions. It also identifies a mutation process between apparently bad and good governance institutions through the implementation of policy (Mahoney and Thelen 2010, 10). In large, multi-tier political systems, where inconsistencies and paradoxes between processes and outcomes are more commonplace, the implementation gaps and inconsistencies in policy interpretations expose the intermediary actors and operational mechanisms at work during the ongoing process of institutional reform. These actors, the characteristics of their interactions and the mechanisms whereby they interact constitute a new context as well as the driving force for the next reform move in an essentially dynamic and highly contested process towards development.

Heterogeneous Actors, Strategic Interactions, Unintended Consequences

These intermediary mechanisms and the actors therein are central pieces in Johnson's analysis of the recent adoption of a more participatory environmental governance framework in China. Johnson (2014) starts with a puzzle which appears to be the opposite to that of Painter's: why should an almighty authoritarian party-state opt for change that will apparently reduce their hold on power? Through his study of the implementation of a new environmental governance framework in China, his answer highlights the role of instrumentalism, strategic interactions and unintended consequences and, like Cheng and Ngo, highlights the implementation and state-scaling dimensions (Swyngedouw 1996). Johnson examines a new legal framework put in place by the central government to improve its capacity over local state and powerful societal actors in meeting central policy targets. Transparency and public participation – the formal objectives of the environmental governance reforms – were not to be fostered as an end, but tolerated in order to co-opt new societal players as allies of the central political executive as deemed necessary or expedient. With this background of the newly enshrined environmental governance framework, as an instrument to an old, traditional administrative problem – improving compliance by local state actors and reducing the implementation gap in policy – there is little surprise in witnessing the haphazard mixes of collaboration and tension between the central state, local agents and societal activists that have evolved subsequently.

By highlighting the instrumentalism of the "good governance program" in Chinese environmental policy, Johnson reminds us that the good governance discourse in Chinese policy circles is embedded in Chinese domestic concerns or, in Painter's terms, "home-grown" rationales. While international learning and influence is apparent in the explicit use of the concept "good governance" (triggered by its translation into Chinese for the 1992 World Bank Report *Governance and Development* (World Bank 1992)), the emphasis has always been on elite domestic needs – how the concept might better serve domestic political objectives, rather than on abstract arguments as to the global applicability of a template of good governance institutions. The preoccupation has been to improve local environment bureau policy compliance. A new public supervisory mechanism was introduced to enlist interested public and groups as allies of the central government in checking local officials. The emerging environmental non-governmental organisations (ENGOs) welcomed this "state-sponsored" role in order to extend the political space for civil society activism. The NIMBY (not-in-my-backyard) activists also made use of official promises on the public supervision mechanism to achieve their objectives to attack unpopular government decisions. Objectively, the instrumental good governance agenda of the Ministry of Environmental Protection (MEP) served three purposes: MEP used good governance rhetoric to achieve better oversight over local environment officials; NIMBYs sought to stop unwanted projects near their neighbour-hoods; ENGOs were eager to extend the space for citizen activism and public participation in environmental policy.

Instability abounded in the interplay of these heterogeneous objectives and processes. The instrumental view of MEP dictates that the public participation reform it initiated was a half-baked one from the beginning, with ambivalent definitions to, say, the boundary of "the public" with whom the authorities should consult before making relevant decisions. The ENGOs' interest in developing institutional propriety over the medium–long term made some ENGOs vulnerable to self-censorship, as they sought to maintain a dialogue with the government. While the NIMBYs employed the rhetoric of public participation in their campaigns, ironically they often did not trust the channels they were defending. The picture is a dynamic one as the ambiguity left in rules and cultivated by various actors for their respective purposes serves also as the platform for change, as each adapts their actions incrementally in response to those of others.

Courts and Education

A system of empowered courts with professional and impartial judges is usually seen as a core institutional fixture in the global good governance template. Also highly placed is the value of equity in the provision of important public goods such as school education, whether as an end and value in itself (education as part of social development), or as a means to economic well-being (education as conducive to economic development). Through com-parative studies, Dressel's (2014) study on courts and politics in Asia and Li and Wang's (2014) on education equity in China and the United States add details and weight to the core message of this feature section: historical contexts vary as they define and shape the shifting dynamics in various governance reforms and development aspirations in different societies.

There are many faces of an empowered judiciary and multiple interpretations of equity in school education policy and practice. The nuances are found across societies and political systems and within each society at certain times and over time. Understanding the variations *within* a society is essential to a deeper appreciation of the character of the society and thus of the variations and similarities *across* societies.

Any effort to define a list of "necessary" or "good-enough" good governance institu-tions will likely rank an independent system of courts high. Courts and judges have long been said to be the necessary building blocks to the rule of law, which in turn is instrumental to bringing about an accountable and stable government. Dressel's analysis of the growing prominence of courts in Asian polities problematises this widespread claim, and suggests that it is overly simplistic to assume any necessary linkage between the development of courts as an institution and the quality of governance generally.

What follows from the traditional confidence in the courts, logically, is that the development of an independent and professional judiciary will work, by and large, in favour of good governance as an outcome. In the case of transitional societies, the development of a strong and active judiciary should, thus, always be beneficial. Dressel's varied empirical cases suggest that characteristics in the broader political system and in particular the other branches of the government are crucial to understanding the significance of the courts. An apparently similar phenomenon, like the increase in "activeness" in the courts, may in fact involve widely different political processes and thus varied interpretations to its meaning for the power, and the role, of the courts in public affairs, as in the contrasting cases of Korea and Thailand. At the same time, the organisational practices and cultural norms within the judiciary can incur a major impact on the behaviour of judges irrespective of the character of the judiciary as an organisation, as in Japan where judges are conservative despite high institutional autonomy of the courts.

Pinning down causation links between the institutional characteristics and judicial actions is tricky, as developments in the courts cannot be analysed in isolation, nor understood as a static feature of a political system. The interaction between the court and its judges and political elites in other branches of the government is highly important to how the court performs in politics and governance. Affecting these interactions are the practice, culture and agency of the judges, as well as those of actors in the executive and legislative branches, and civil society. Dressel drives home the point that diversities abound even in a single arena. Understanding the diversity of the courts hinges upon our understanding of other institutions and of their interactions.

In comparing education reforms in China and the United States, Li and Wang (2014) return to a basic question: why should governments infamous for their "bad governance" adopt good governance institutions and practices? When they do, does an apparently similar institution mean the same, in terms of its impacts for governance, as that practiced in the advanced economies? The accounts of reforms given in this feature section have stressed the importance of understanding the micro-processes at the actors' level and explaining the adoption of governance reforms from the perspective of the host, not donor, countries. Through the overview of reform processes in the United States and China, Li and Wang highlight the similarities as well as differences in their reform logics. In particular, the development of equity standards and practices in education is found to be, similarly, a product-in-the-making in both countries despite the large differences in their political systems and economies. Their reform processes also exhibit parallels. At the same time, obvious differences in history and institutions do matter. The courts played a more conspicuous role in the US *vis-à-vis* the political executive in China in the processes of education policy change. Major differences have also remained in the policy discourse in the two societies, with the theme of local control taking more of a back seat in discussions (but not in political practice) in China.

Education equity concerns in both countries first sprang from dissatisfaction over wide disparities in government funding in different territorial jurisdictions. Policy strategies were subsequently devised to reduce the funding gaps either through regulation or direct fiscal subsidies. The inter-governmental dimension has loomed large in this process. The states are the traditional players in the US reform, whilst the federal government is also increasingly drawn in; in China, the central and provincial governments have supplied additional funding to schools. Problems arise, however, as the quest for education equity brings new heat to old concerns over competing values, in this case the competition between equity and efficiency objectives. Local governments and schools welcome the new resources to address the equity gap, but they detest the additional strings and increased oversight that come with the resources. Difficulties in implementation (for example, where and how to draw the line for capping) and stakeholders' resistance have led both countries to turn to an absolute standard of adequacy in place of equalisation.

The meaning of equity in education and what constitutes an appropriate reform strategy have been in a constant flux, reflecting the results of the shifting concerns of equity and efficiency as they evolve, differentially, in the historical conditions in both countries. The larger message from this US-China comparison over school education equity responds to criticism of the good governance agenda: reforms are *not* only for the consumption of the developing societies. "Late developers" have been urged to emulate measures in advanced economies, and the underlying ahistorical view of development has been much criticised. Lately, as we noted earlier, this position is further weakened by economic crises in the advanced economies. By comparing the historical experience of US and China over several decades, Li and Wang (2014) press the point that the similar challenges we meet in seeking good governance and development, as outcome, in *both* the developing and advanced societies are more of a routine common experience. Recognising this fact is important: we all have a lot to learn from each other on our similar yet diverse trajectories to *better* governance and development.

Conclusion

We set out in this feature section to join an important discussion: how to interpret, and to improve, the international and domestic efforts on good governance institutional reforms geared towards development. This discussion has gained additional leverage as a result of the recent economic crisis in the advanced economies, which ironically highlighted how little we understand the role of institutions in development, not to say master the institutional reform process to further development. The five papers that follow this introductory essay seek to contribute to the discussion by telling a number of stories – where, in a number of Asian societies, actual institutional reforms have taken place with varied effects on development. We have stressed the importance of not assuming the relevance of a fixed template of institutions across societies, since actual conditions in these societies matter, and the conditions often vary immensely across societies, as well as within a society across time. However our objective is *not* to rule out international learning of any sort, as it might still be practically beneficial to start from some commonly used *good* practices, but to make use of any suggested best practice wisely. To achieve this goal, the key is to appreciate fully how actual conditions make a difference to the linkage between governance institutions and development, and that actual conditions in different societies align as well as differ.

Notes

[1] Marking the onset of the agenda is the publication of the World Bank (1989) report, *Sub-Saharan Africa: From Crisis to Sustainable Growth*, in 1989, which attributes Africa's development problems in the 1980s to a "crisis in governance" (see Leftwich 1993; Gibbon 1993).

[2] In the case of World Bank/IMF loans, political conditionality is often indirectly effected through connectivity to bilateral aid, on which political conditionality can be imposed, given the explicit prohibition against political conditionality in their charters (Gibbon 1993, 55–56).

[3] The IMF conference on "Macro and Growth Policies in the Wake of the Crisis" on 7–8 March 2011 (http://www.imf.org/external/np/seminars/eng/2011/res/index.htm) was hosted by four top economists, including two Nobel laureates: Michael Spence (Stanford), Joseph Stiglitz (Columbia, and former Chief Economist of World Bank), Olivier Blanchard (Director of Research at IMF), and David Romer (California, Berkeley). Attendees

included leading policy-makers and academics from both the advanced and emerging economies, and people from civil society and industry.

[4] See Rodan, Hewison, and Robison (2006) for a critical review of the three theoretical approaches to political economy: neoclassical economics, historical institutionalism and social conflict theory. The Good Governance Agenda falls within the paradigm of the neoclassical approach.

[5] See Gibbon (1993) for a telling account of the politics of aid in the World Bank up to the early 1990s.

[6] One reason for the reluctance to embrace political conditionality outright in the World Bank and the IMF is organisational concern: their formal charters contain explicit references against an overt political role. The result is what Doornbos (2001, 95) describes as a "curious" situation: "while…in principle comprising a political dimension, in actuality the use of 'governance' on the donor front…seemed to imply a certain depoliticisation of political processes."

[7] This has led some to explicitly ascribe a "politico-ethical orientation" to the concept (Preston 1982, 17).

[8] The plurality of meanings of the concept is more readily recognised by those premising the political dimension of life in development, so that meanings will vary to reflect the shifting contours of politics across time and space (Leftwich 2000, 69). Chapters 2 and 3 of Leftwich (2000) concisely summarise the major strands of conceptions of development in recent decades.

[9] See the papers in the special issue on "Neo-liberal Development Policy in Asia Beyond the Post-Washington Consensus," *Journal of Contemporary Asia* 42(3) (2012), and especially the papers by Carroll (2012a, 2012b), Cammack (2012) for the rich literature on the neoliberal state.

[10] The property rights institutions and contracting institutions are perhaps the two "essential" sets of institutions that most people would agree have a positive role on economic development, cutting across variations in other conditions in varying contexts (North 1981; Acemoglu and Johnson 2005).

References

Acemoglu, D., and S. Johnson. 2005. "Unbundling Institutions." *Journal of Political Economy* 113 (5): 949–995.

Acemoglu, D., S. Johnson, and J. Robinson. 2005. "Institutions as a Fundamental Cause of Long-Run Growth." In *Handbook of Economic Gmwth, Volume IA*, edited by P. Aghion and S. Durlanf, 385–472. Amsterdam: Elsevier.

Andrews, M. 2008. "Good Government Means Different Things in Different Countries." Faculty Research Working Papers Series, RWP08-68. Cambridge, MA: Harvard Kennedy School. https://research.hks.harvard.edu/publications/getFile.aspx?Id=324

Blanchard, O. 2011. "The Future of Macroeconomic Policy: Nine Tentative Conclusions." IMF (International Monetary Fund). Accessed August 13, 2012. http://blog-imfdirect.imf.org/2011/03/13/future-of-macroeconomic-policy/.

Cammack, P. 2012. "Risk, Social Protection and the World Market." *Journal of Contemporary Asia* 42 (3): 359–377.

Carroll, T. 2012a. "Introduction: Neo-Liberal Development Policy in Asia Beyond the Post-Washington Consensus." *Journal of Contemporary Asia* 42 (3): 350–358.

Carroll, T. 2012b. "Working on, Through and Around the State: The Deep Marketisation of Development in the Asia-Pacific." *Journal of Contemporary Asia* 42 (3): 378–404.

Cheng, Yi.-W., and T.-W. Ngo. 2014. "The Heterodoxy of Governance Under Decentralization: Rent-Seeking Politics in China's Tobacco Growing Areas." *Journal of Contemporary Asia* 44 (2): 221–240.

Coorey, S. 2012. "Growing Institutions? Grow the People!" Accessed August 13, 2012. http://www.imfdirect.imf.org/2012/08/10/growing-institutions-grow-the-people/ .

Demmers, J., A. Fernández Jilberto, and B. Hogenboom, eds. 2004. *Good Governance in the Era of Global Neoliberalism: Conflict and Depoliticisation in Latin America, Eastern Europe, Asia and Europe and Africa.* London: Routledge.

Doornbos, M. 1995. "State Formation Processes Under External Supervision: Reflections on 'Good Governance'." In *Aid and Political Conditionality*, edited by O. Stokke, 371–391. London: Frank Cass.

Doornbos, M. 2001. "'Good Governance': The Rise and Decline of a Policy Metaphor." *Journal of Development Studies* 37 (6): 93–108.

Dressel, B. 2014. "Governance, Courts and Politics in Asia." *Journal of Contemporary Asia* 44 (2): 259–278.

Engerman, S., and K. Sokoloff. 2008. "Debating the Role of Institutions in Political and Economic Development: Theory, History and Findings." *American Review of Political Science* 11: 119–135.

Evans, P. 1995. *Embedded Autonomy: States and Industrial Transformation.* Princeton: Princeton University Press.

Gibbon, P. 1993. "The World Bank and the New Politics of Aid." In *Political Conditionality*, edited by G. Sorensen, 35–62. London: Frank Cass.

Glaseser, E., R. La Porta, F. Lopez-De-Silanes, and A. Shleifer. 2004. "Do Institutions Cause Growth?." *Journal of Economic Growth* 9 (1): 271–303.

Goldsmith, A. 2007. "Is Governance Reform a Catalyst for Development." *Governance* 20 (2): 165–186.

Grindle, M. 2004. "Good Enough Governance: Poverty Reduction and Reform in Developing Countries." *Governance: An International Journal of Policy, Administration, and Institutions* 17 (4): 525–548.

Hyden, G., J. Court, and K. Mease, eds. 2004. *Making Sense of Governance: Empirical Evidence From Sixteen Developing Countries*. London: Lynne Rienner.

International Monetary Fund. 2012. "IMF Launches Institute for Capacity Development", Press Release No. 12/156, May 1, 2012. Accessed July 15, 2012. http://www.imf.org/external/np/sec/pr/2012/pr12156.htm.

Johnson, C. 1995. *Japan, Who Governs? the Rise of the Developmental State*. New York: Norton.

Johnson, T. 2014. "Good Governance for Environmental Protection in China: Instrumentation, Strategic Interactions, and Unintended Consequences." *Journal of Contemporary Asia* 44 (2): 241–258.

King, P. 1995. "Historical Contextualism: The New Historicism?." *History of European Ideas* 21 (2): 208–233.

Leftwich, A. 1993. "Governance, Democracy and Development in the Third World." *Third World Quarterly* 14 (3): 605–624.

Leftwich, A. 2000. *States of Development: On the Primacy of Politics in Development*. Cambridge: Polity Press.

Li, L. 2009. *Towards Responsible Government in East Asia: Trajectories, Intentions and Meanings*. London: Routledge.

Li, L., and W. Wang. 2014. "Pursuing Equity in Education: Conflicting Views and Shifting Strategies." *Journal of Contemporary Asia* 44 (2): 279–297.

Mahoney, J., and K. Thelen. 2010. "A Theory of Gradual Institutional Change." In *Explaining Institutional Change: Ambiguity, Agency and Power*, edited by J. Mahoney and K. Thelen, 1–37. Cambridge: Cambridge University Press.

North, D. 1981. *Structure and Change in Economic History*. New York: Norton.

Painter, M. 2002. "Making Sense of Good Governance." *Public Administration and Policy* 11 (2): 77–100.

Painter, M. 2014. "Governance Reforms in China and Vietnam: Marketisation, Leapfrogging and Retro-Fitting." *Journal of Contemporary Asia* 44 (2): 204–220.

Pierson, P. 2004. *Politics in Time: History, Institutions, and Social Analysis*. Princeton: Princeton University Press.

Preston, P. 1982. *Theories of Development*. London: Routedge.

Przeworski, A. 2004. "Institutions Matter?." *Government and Opposition* 39 (4): 527–540.

Rodan, G., K. Hewison, and R. Robison. 2006. "Theorizing Markets in South-East Asia: Power and Contestation." In *The Political Economy of South-East Asia: Markets, Power and Contestation*, edited by G. Rodan, K. Hewison, and R. Robison, 1–38. Oxford: Oxford University Press.

Sachs, J. 2003. "Institutions Don't Rule: Direct Effects of Geography on Per Capita Income." Working Paper 9490. Cambridge: National Bureau of Economic Research. http://www.nber.org/papers/w9490

Sørensen, G., ed. 1993. *Political Conditionality*. London: Frank Cass.

Stein, H., and E. Nafziger. 1991. "Structural Adjustment, Human Needs, and the World Bank Agenda." *The Journal of Modern African Studies* 29 (1): 173–189.

Stewart, J. 1985. "Dilemmas." In *Between Centre and Locality*, edited by S. Ranson, G. Jones and K. Walsh, 23–35. London: George Allen and Unwin.

Stokke, O. 1995a. "Aid and Political Conditionality: Core Issues and State of the Art." In *Aid and Political Conditionality*, edited by O. Stokke, 1–87. London: Frank Cass.

Stokke, O., ed. 1995b. *Aid and Political Conditionality*. London: Frank Cass.

Swyngedouw, E. 1996. "Restructuring Citizenship, the Re-Scaling of the State and the New Authoritarianism: Closing the Belgian Mines." *Urban Studies* 33 (8): 1499–1521.

Törnquist, O. 1999. *Politics and Development: A Critical Introduction*. London: Sage.

Woo-Cumings, M., ed. 1999. *The Developmental State*. Ithaca: Cornell University Press.

World Bank. 1981. *Accelerated Development*. Washington, DC: World Bank.

World Bank. 1989. *Sub-Saharan Africa: From Crisis to Sustainable Growth*. Washington, DC: World Bank.

World Bank. 1992. *Governance and Development*. Washington, DC: World Bank.

Xia, M. 1997. "The Two-Tier Developmental State: Institutionalization of Provincial Legislatures, Development Strategy, and Market-Creation in China, 1980–95." PhD Diss., Temple University. Philadelphia.

Governance Reforms in China and Vietnam: Marketisation, Leapfrogging and Retro-Fitting

MARTIN PAINTER

Department of Public Policy, City University of Hong Kong, Kowloon, Hong Kong

ABSTRACT *International good governance orthodoxy proposes a set of step-by-step governance reforms as a necessary component of development. However, this orthodox view is more a reflection of persistent myths of development than of its realities. Living examples of this are found in contemporary China and Vietnam. In these two authoritarian one-party states, much international orthodoxy of good governance reform and practice is deliberately contradicted in the reform and opening-up process. In uncovering the underlying political logic of persistent "lag" in governance reforms in Vietnam and China, we observe examples of leapfrogging and retro-fitting, rather than orderly sequencing of governance reforms. The case of rapid marketisation of public service delivery is used to illustrate the arguments. The lesson is clear: good governance can come later.*

China and Vietnam are both transition economies (that is, transiting from a command to an open market economy) but remain authoritarian states under Communist Party rule. Both governments score low on "good governance" indices while experiencing dramatic economic growth and impressive levels of poverty reduction. Meanwhile, administrative reform is high on the agenda but the intentions are ambiguous and the outcomes mixed. Measures such as anti-corruption, civil service and transparency reforms receive particularly unfavourable comments from international observers and good governance advocates. Even where there has been change, observers often note "missed steps" in the process and "incompatible" layering of new measures onto existing institutions, in particular the institutions of the communist one-party state.

The desirability of good governance reforms for developing countries has become a defining orthodoxy of contemporary international aid and development discourses. The package is familiar: rule of law, transparency and accountability, anti-corruption, merit-based civil service reforms and so on. But there are many reasons to doubt the relevance of some of these orthodox prescriptions to developing countries. One such reason is a lack of capacity and resources for implementing complex reforms; another stems from the many pitfalls, including cultural tensions or incompatibilities, of implementing "decontextualised" models and prescriptions. These objections might be dealt with by lowering ambitions, paying more attention to local stakeholders and lengthening time-horizons, without jettisoning the basic model. But a more fundamental objection stems from the fact that Western experience tells us that good governance is not a pre-requisite for development. That is, underlying the good governance narrative is a sequencing fallacy.

Nowhere is this better illustrated that in contemporary China and Vietnam which, according to the orthodox model, are ignoring some good governance principles alto-gether and, rather than proceeding in an orderly, step-by-step manner, are deliberately leapfrogging. In this context, both the prevalence and persistence of bad governance in China and Vietnam are best understood as embedded in these governments' chosen development trajectories. A case in point is the aggressive marketisation of public service delivery mechanisms as part of the transition. From a good governance perspective this arguably was not a good idea – it was "premature" and "out of sequence." But this is increasingly well understood by local reformers and there are growing efforts to deal with the adverse consequences (uneven access, corruption and quality deficits). In sum, in terms of sequencing, good governance can be "retro-fitted."

In elaborating on this argument, we turn first to a more detailed exposition of the sequencing fallacies of the good governance model. Next, we look at the nature of the commitment to public administration reform by governments in China and Vietnam, before exploring the reasons for the reform strategies and the logics they followed in the case of public service delivery reforms. While these reforms bear a strong resemblance to recent New Public Management (NPM) prescriptions in the West, the details of the case show how the circumstances and pressures facing reformers were such that a "transition-specific" reform logic and agenda emerged: the priority was to use the market to unburden the command economy state of responsibilities, while accelerating service production. A decline in governance standards occurred in the process and was tolerated for the time being as a by-product of the reform strategy. Significantly, however, as the concluding section shows, there is now in motion a set of reforms that have grown out of the reform logics already in place, seeking to remedy some of the worst problems. Elements of good governance may be coming, but not until later.

Sequencing Fallacies and Good Governance

As Peerenboom (2009, 1) writes, "[s]equencing has recently become a bad word in development studies." He is referring specifically to the contention arising from debate on whether democracy or development should come first (Carothers 2007). Peerenboom focuses his discussion on rule of law and institutional reform (as distinct from democra-tisation) and we shall follow his example. Within the governance and development literature and among international development actors there is a strong presumption that good governance is a pre-requisite for development. Good governance is characteristically associated with some key institutions – for example:

> Good governance is epitomized by predictable, open and enlightened policymaking (that is, transparent processes); a bureaucracy imbued with professional ethos; an executive arm of government accountable for its actions; and a strong civil society

participating in public affairs; and all behaving under the rule of law (World Bank 1994, vii).

The blueprint is perhaps best viewed as a doctrinal distillation of imagined Western, liberal-democratic historical experience (Painter 2002). It fails to depict reality in two main ways: first, it mistakes a model for the real thing (no developed country actually conforms to the good governance model); and second, it misreads history and makes unsustainable propositions about sequencing.

As to the first issue, Andrews (2010) has pointed out that no successful, developed economy is actually governed in the manner that the "best practice" good governance models advocate. What we observe in reality among the leaders in the "effective government" league tables is considerable variety, including in some of the core features of the model. For example, in some governments, political patronage in appointments to the bureaucracy or to key government agencies is rare, while in others political appointments are the norm; in some "exemplar" countries, legislators play havoc with rule-bound administration, while in others bureaucrats keep them at bay; some governments are highly open, others very secretive, and so on. With respect to financial management, where it has long been argued that there is a broad international consensus on what constitutes "best practice," effective governments are not any more likely to adopt these practices; indeed, they vary in their adoption or lack of adoption even more than do the laggards, many of whom have swallowed them hook, line and sinker (Andrews 2010). In a similar vein, Brinkerhoff and Goldsmith (2005) have pointed out that what they label "institutional dualism" – coexistence of both "good" and "bad" governance institutions and practices – is still plainly evident in most contemporary developed countries.

As to the second objection concerning sequencing, the reading of development underlying the good governance narrative ignores the fact that, in practice, the sequencing implied was not universally part of Western historical experience. For example, economic take-off in the USA occurred well in advance of the realisation of institutional reforms now associated with good governance (Goldsmith 2007). Only later did the progressive movement agitate for reform. An obvious example of this kind of "retro-fitting" of good governance was the "late" arrival of freedom of information legislation in the last decades of the twentieth century in most Western democracies (Sweden being a notable exception). Advocating transparency as a key part of the development agenda ignores a venerable tradition of opacity in the public administration of most rich countries.

Cross-national data on development and good governance drives this point home. Much effort has been devoted to developing indices that specify empirically testable "quality of government" attributes and their correlations with development. The indices include "voice and accountability," "rule of law," "control of corruption," "regulatory quality" and the like. Numerous cross-national studies have used these indices to investigate whether such attributes are associated with high growth, high income and well-being. One survey of this literature (Holmberg, Rothstein, and Nasiritousi 2008, 19) showed that a few measures (the World Bank's "Government Effectiveness" and "Rule of Law" Indices and Transparency International's "Corruptions Perception" Index) are highly inter-correlated and have "very strong" correlations with gross domestic product (GDP). But at the same time they have "positive but *surprisingly weak* (my emphasis) correlations with economic growth." Although rich countries score high on indicators of good governance, the role that was played by institutional reform in becoming rich does not come through from the data. Khan (2007) shows from his data that countries that grew fastest in the late twentieth century demonstrated no significant differences in terms of enjoying the benefits of having a range of "good governance" institutions. The effectiveness of rule of law or any other set of governance institutions cannot be claimed to be a causal factor from these cross-national data. Holmberg, Rothstein, and Nasiritousi (2008, 19) conclude that "the causality between economic growth and quality of government is more like a 'virtuous circle,'" where the institutional and developmental trajectories may be intertwined but no clear lessons can be drawn about causation or sequencing (see also Goldsmith 2007). Peerenboom (2009, 9) makes a similar point: rich countries tend to have institutions that are characterised by the "rule of law" label, but maybe they got that way after they grew, not before. Analyses of developmental success stories in East Asia show the importance of the role of the state for economic development, but just what the governance ingredients were was highly context-dependent, varying from case to case and depending on appropriate applications rather than a single template (Khan 2007). Moreover, many factors apart from public policy settings and institutional frameworks were important.

In sum, there is no firm basis in these data on which to recommend to any set of reformers a specific set of good governance reforms as a prerequisite for development. As Grindle (2004, 526) argues, the bundling together of a range of attributes of good governance, showing that they express positive correlations with various desirable outcomes, is of no help in telling reformers "what is essential and what's not, what should come first and what should follow...." Nevertheless, the search for temporal as well as logical relationships between good governance and development remains a feature of discussions in the international public administration and development community, where there is often a concern for the sequencing of reforms. On the one hand, the argument that "A" must come before "B" is often just good common sense – for example, you cannot introduce a sound system of financial audit without first training and employing some auditors. In the field of public finance, the orthodox approach is to distinguish between "basic reforms" such as complete budget coverage, consolidated Treasury accounts and adequate budget controls, and "advanced" reforms such as performance-oriented budgeting and fiscal transparency (Tandberg and Pavesic-Skerlep 2009). More broadly, the World Bank advised "choosing and sequencing public sector reforms carefully, in line with initial capacities, to create firmer ground for further reform" (World Bank 2003, 194).

Often, sequencing claims also depict governance reforms marching in step with wider social and economic developments. A classic and highly influential argument along these lines is Schick's (1998) contention that New Zealand's pioneering NPM reforms have only limited relevance to developing countries. Government by contract and "output steering" depend upon formality and legality prevailing, both in the public and private sectors so that accurate monitoring and effective enforcement are possible. In developing countries, informality is the norm: until the rule of law governs market transactions and government administration alike, contractualism as a basis for public sector reform will not work. Schick (1998, 129) proposes that reform in these countries should proceed through "a logical sequence of steps that diminish the scope of informality while building managerial capacity, confidence, and experience." He argues that developing countries need a rule-bound neutral, professional, centralised Weberian-style bureaucracy and firmly established basic public sector budgeting and accounting procedures *before* they can safely introduce more decentralised, market-mimicking models of public service delivery. Schick's conclusions have been echoed by the World Bank: "[f]irst stage reforms" should aim to achieve or strengthen "formality, discipline and compliance with the rules," while second-stage reforms (after a "formality threshold" has been reached) should aim to "strengthen flexibility, discretion and a focus on results." In the case of civil service reform, "first-stage reform" requires "creat[ing] a legally defined cadre with common terms and conditions," following which "second-stage" reforms can be introduced, such as "…devolv[ing] and diversify[ing] pay arrangements to provide flexibility to employers" (World Bank 2003, 194–196). The same message is delivered in the case of sectoral reforms such as telecommunications, where establishing pro-competitive regulatory regimes in advance of privatising state monopolies has been shown to produce better results (Wallsten 2002).

As it happens, reformers in China and Vietnam in addressing public service delivery problems seem to have ignored these words of advice and gone about things in the wrong order. As discussed below, this is part of a more general pattern of heterodoxy in relation to good governance doctrines. Nevertheless, some "corrective measures" are being taken to address the governance shortcomings of rapid marketisation in the public sector: the "wrong sequence" as it turns out may be just a *different* sequence to the one prescribed. That is, Schick may be basically correct in his common-sense statement of the need for certain capacities to be in place before a marketised public service delivery system can be effectively implemented, but wrong in suggesting that there is only one sequence in which this can be achieved. Leapfrogging and retro-fitting may in some circumstances be sensible reform strategies.

Public Sector Reforms in China and Vietnam

China began its "reform era" some years earlier than Vietnam, which launched its "renovation" programme or *doi moi* in 1986. Both countries embarked on a process of marketisation of their economies. The scope of reforms to the state sector associated with these changes has been far-reaching. On the one hand, they have involved economic restructuring – dismantling the command economy; and on the other hand they have involved administrative restructuring – creating new organisations and procedures for regulating the market sector. Important legal reforms have accompanied these changes. One basic governance issue lies behind the reforms: how to construct new kinds of state capacity in a market environment. While there are some differences in emphases and in implementation style between the two countries, there are strong similarities in prioritisation and sequencing.

To begin with, there have been successive re-structuring and downsizing reforms as part of the process of dismantling the Soviet-style state instrumentalities that directly controlled the command economy, resulting in a new focus on regulation and coordination, away from direct economic micro-management (Dong, Christensen, and Painter 2010a; Ngok and Chan 2003; Yang 2004). As well, new laws, ordinances, circulars and other documents have been written to regulate non-state activity. In the process of legal and institutional reform, steps have been taken to reduce the burden of unnecessary controls on the economy encouraged by the old "permissions" or "begging-and-giving" culture and to formalise and clarify administrative procedures. Due process and legality are seen as instruments for developing more reliable administrative controls under the party's leadership. At the same time, neither in China nor in Vietnam are legal institutions viewed as occupying an autonomous sphere separate from the party-state. In this, as in other ways, "rule by law" does not equate with Western notions of "rule of law" (Gillespie 2005, 2006; Peerenboom 2004).

State-owned enterprises (SOEs) have been restructured to enable them to act as commercially driven bodies in the market place. An increasing number have been "equitised," "socialised" or "privatised" (although this last word tends to be avoided in the local discourses). Subsidies and micro-management by the state have been curtailed, although many SOEs retain privileged access to loans, land and administrative clearances (Broadman 2001; Fforde 2005; Yang 2004). In parallel, public service delivery units of all kinds (particularly in the cities) have been "pushed into the market," required to charge user fees and set free to compete for customers. For example, many education and health services in China and Vietnam are now managed and provided by lightly regulated "para-state" entities with limited budget subsidy. Much of this process has been piecemeal rather than carefully designed, although reformers have paid lip-service to NPM models in their rationales (Gu and Zhang 2006; London 2006; Li 2011).

Closely related to these measures is extensive administrative and fiscal decentralisation. Local governments have had to "look to the market" for revenue rather than rely on central budgets or taxes, and as a result they have gained some autonomy from the centre. In this process, distortions in local tax regimes have occurred (Dong, Christensen, and Painter 2010b; Duckett 2001; Lu 2000). Financial management devolution has been motivated primarily by shifting the administrative and financial burden to the local unit and thence (via fees and charges) to the client or customer. Periods of "turning a blind eye" to informal off-budget activities alternate with clamp-downs to regulate abuses, such as the measures in China in the early 2000s to reduce the "peasant's burden" by abolishing rural fees and charges (Lu 2000; Wedeman 2000; World Bank 2005b).

"Civil service" reform has been high on the agenda in both countries, including new laws and regulations to formalise public employment. In both China and Vietnam the principle has been maintained that the ruling Communist Party is ultimately in full control of the appointment and promotion of all public officials. However, criteria for promotion among party leaders and state managers at all levels increasingly combine technical with political performance evaluations. Meanwhile, salary reform has "monetised" remuneration but not seriously attempted to link reward with performance (Burns 2001; Chan 2004; Painter 2003, 2006).

There have been extensive campaigns against corruption, largely using pre-existing Soviet-style inspection and enforcement machinery and citizen complaint mechanisms. However, the fundamental issue of tackling systemic corruption within the party remains unresolved. The party will not accept external, independent oversight and continues to control anti-corruption campaigns (Gillespie 2002; Gong 2006, 2008). But at the same time, steps have been taken to make local officials more accountable to citizens. "Citizen's Report Cards," "Citizen Charters" and "one-stop-shops" have promoted transparency and citizen accountability in the processing of routine business (Foster 2005; Li 2002; Oi and Rozelle 2000). However, official corruption and abuses of power at the local level remain major grievances, resulting in frequent protests which create continuing anxiety within the party in both countries.

Although this brief summary does not exhaust all the areas of reform and change, it encompasses the most significant. The reform agenda is comprehensive and generates frequent major announcements of new measures by the top leadership. Much of the reform discourse echoes global reform themes such as deregulation, devolution and transparency. Although borrowing is evident in China, much of it is at the level of myths and symbols and takes the form of "superstitious learning" (Dong, Christensen, and Painter 2010a). In Vietnam, an active donor community provides technical and financial resources, along with a stream of advice about good governance. However, good governance advocates are mostly disappointed with the record to date: for example, politicisation continues to trump impartiality and legality at many crucial points; transparency and public accountability are limited by party control; considerations of service quality, accountability and access are inhibited by the lack of a "service" or "performance" culture; and so on. In terms of what actually has changed, the outcomes do not show a steady or significant improvement in key governance practices. The implementation gaps and shortfalls are the biggest where the deficiencies are most glaring. Basic building-blocks of good governance practice are left unreformed amidst a hectic agenda of transformations in other aspects of public administration.

But these criticisms only make sense within a decontextualised frame of reference. The Chinese and Vietnamese reform programmes have their own logic when viewed in context. The events set in motion by the decision to dismantle the command economy and hasten the creation of markets have produced a set of circumstances, including unintended consequences, that shape and constrain the decisions of actors and hence what kind of reform is feasible. Where convenient and appropriate, reformers have called on external models to support the changes, but just as often they have found their own "home-grown" rationales. In many cases, they have been driven as much by bottom-up developments as by top-down models. The remainder of the paper takes as a case study one such field of reform where a mix of local circumstances, overseas models and home-grown solutions has driven the agenda: the privatisation of many areas of public service delivery.

Decentralisation and the Informalisation of Local Bureaucratic Power

The purpose of this section is to set out the wider context of the changing role of the state during the transition process, as a prelude to the analysis of service delivery reforms. The state has decentralised in two senses: first, because many former state entities have been "pushed into the market" and second because this has fed back into a growing dispersal of power to the periphery *within* the state. One important aspect of this has been the opportunistic behaviour of public officials when engaging as market actors. Public officials, acting at first from *within* the state, have occupied new economic and political roles *beyond* the state as they participated in and benefitted from the dispersal of the state's resources into the market economy. Gainsborough (2003) described how a "state business interest," with strong roots in provincial and local party-state circles, emerged as a powerful political force in Vietnam during the 1990s, with largely centrifugal effects (Beresford 2001; Fforde 1993; Gainsborough 2003, 72). Informal and illegal uses of state power and resources to facilitate economic accumulation have been evident during official programmes of state restructuring while, in turn, being major forces in shaping that restructuring. "Reform" has often been captured by local party-state economic actors for their own purposes, creating major challenges for the national governments of China and

Vietnam in responding to widespread public discontent over corruption and abuses of power.

Decentralisation has also entailed growth in the functions of sub-national government. In both China and Vietnam, there has been a trend towards a greater sub-national share in service delivery and expenditure. In China, sub-national expenditures rose from about 45% of the total prior to the economic reforms in the 1980s to close to 70%. The accumulation of such responsibilities at local level stimulated a rapid growth in local bureaucracies – in China sub-national official employment grew by nearly 80% between 1978 and 1987 (Shirk 1992, 85). At the same time, the taxing capacity of local governments did not keep up (Mountfield and Wong 2005, 97), with the result that local governments turned to "extra-budgetary" sources to make up the shortfall. Speculative land deals became a major source of local government revenue. In the process, the growing weakness of the centre in regulating local government behaviour was revealed. A plethora of fees, charges, levies and fines were imposed by local officials, many of them of dubious legality (Bernstein and Lu 2003, 107–109). The result was an escalation of extra-budget and off-budget revenues and expenditures, estimated to amount to up to half of total local government expenditures (Mountfield and Wong 2005, 98).[1] These sources of revenue were tapped through the use of local discretionary powers; were retained by the local bodies that collected them; and were available to reward local officials with jobs, bonuses and other benefits (Bernstein and Lu 2003; Gong 2006; Wedeman 2000). Local audit and tax offices took a forgiving view of irregularities and adopted a pragmatic approach to punishment (Oi 1999, 153–159). Clamp-downs by the centre did not always achieve the desired results. Similar processes of informalisation, coupled with half-hearted oversight and regulation, were evident in Vietnam (Painter 2006).

The growth of off-budget activity was directly associated with strengthening the autonomy of service delivery agencies and the spawning of new ones to manage development and to deliver services. These processes were particularly significant in the developing cities, rather than in rural areas, where state subsidies were still needed to maintain the viability of service providers (but were often not forthcoming). Again, this sounds like NPM but really was actually home-grown. Burgeoning numbers of entities on the fringes of the state in areas of rapid development gave new opportunities for employment, enterprise and profit, while not relying on state budgets. Legal personality has been endowed on a new range of "social organisations" under state sponsorship and regulation, many of them performing "state-like" functions. In the process, the state has created a complex array of state-cum-societal organisational "hybrids," some set up with a view to returning profits, others concerned more with "community construction" (Duckett 1998; Benewick, Tong, and Howell 2004). As discussed in the next section, large areas of public service delivery have shifted radically to this "para-state" sector.

Informalisation, Autonomisation and Marketisation

In both China and Vietnam, the administrative organisation of the state had three components: administrative agencies concerned with "state management" (ministries and departments); service delivery units (such as public hospitals); and enterprises. Here, we focus mainly on the second category. China had over one million service delivery units employing nearly 30 million in 2002, or 41% of the public sector workforce. Some 60% of China's professional classes worked for them; they owned two-thirds of "non-commercial" state assets; and they absorbed about one-third of the recurrent expenditures of all governments (World Bank 2005a, 1–2). In practice the way these organisations were staffed and managed differed little from administrative agencies: the same terms and conditions of "civil service" employment and pay scales applied to them (although one difference was that many of their employees were in professional or technical rather than administrative ranks) and party control and management was exercised. They were also likely to be funded (at least in part) from the state budget. Their service functions were diverse, but the largest sectors were education and health. Supervision rested with administrative departments at central, provincial or local levels. In China, 65% of their employees were affiliated with county and township governments. The control and management of service delivery units was a matter of vital interest to local governments, as many were repositories of significant state assets, important instruments of patronage and (increasingly) significant sources of revenue. Many of the burgeoning fees and charges levied by local government bodies referred to earlier were collected at the point of service delivery by these agencies. About half of the revenue of service delivery units in China by 2002 was raised through fees (World Bank 2005a, 3).

In China, reforms and "experiments on a vast scale" (Cheng 2001, 322) to unleash the productive potential of this sector included more flexible systems of recruitment and remuneration such as incentive schemes for employees; separation from government departments; delegation of enhanced management autonomy; and increased powers to levy fees or set charges and to borrow money for investment coupled with new regulations allowing for retention of revenues. In a similar vein in Vietnam, Decree 10 in 2002 formally granted public service delivery units a degree of formal financial management autonomy, including many of the same measures. A major driver of these measures was the need to find a way to cover the cost of retaining state employees in a context of fiscal restraint, as government budgets were increasingly made dependent upon new but limited systems of taxation of firms and citizens.

Thus, like state-owned enterprises, most service delivery units were "pushed into the market." Even where they are supposedly "non-profit," they were expected to recoup their costs and seek out revenue from the "customer." The result is that a market for the service in question was created where one did not formerly exist. For example, in Vietnam, Hanoi schools were permitted to enrol so-called "Grade B" fee-paying students who did not meet academic or residential entrance requirements (World Bank 2005b, 110). All parents paid some fees, but Grade B students incurred a higher fee (on average some three to four times higher). Only a small proportion of the fees charged to enrol these "extra-plan" and "extra-budget" students had to be remitted to the central department. The surplus funds were mostly allocated to the school salary budget for "top-ups." This semi-privatisation of secondary schooling was facilitated and encouraged in Vietnam under regulations which permitted not only "semi-public" classes in state schools but also "semi-public schools" and "people-founded" schools (London 2006). These developments closely followed those already implemented in China. In Shanghai, "publicly-owned privately-run" schools under a contracting-out system became an important part of the sector, with school managers having extensive autonomy in staff hiring, fee collection, student recruitment and so on. By the end of the 1990s government funding accounted for only about 50% of education expenditure in the city and there was a wide variety of organisational forms spanning public and private sectors. In 2003, a Ministry of Education circular sought to regularise a range of activities permitting service delivery units, private individuals and social organisations to set up and manage "independent colleges" as private institutions (Ngok and Chan 2003; World Bank 2005a, 5–6).

Local governments were also encouraged to sponsor the take-up of public service delivery by non-government "social organisations." In China, this resulted in a special category of "civilian-run non-enterprise organisations." Under a set of 1998 regulations, they must register and be overseen by an official or professional "sponsor" organisation. Registration of such bodies has mushroomed. They have been popular, for example, for the provision of old-people's homes on a non-subsidised fee-paying basis, to the extent that the "non-state" sector has become the dominant residential elderly care provider. Residents pay fees and their standard of accommodation and care will depend on their ability to pay (or the benevolence of the owner). The viability of these self-financed entities is precarious but the state has steadfastly sought to avoid subsidy, with other kinds of official support also being minimal (Wong and Tang 2006).

The reform process has thus been a mixture of both informal, bottom-up stratagems and top-down encouragement. Marketisation has suited the interests of important professional groups and of producers, as well as local governments, which have been unburdened of some of the costs of provision. The bottom-up pressures came in part from employees, particularly technical and professional staff, seeking secure jobs and higher incomes. In both Vietnam and China, official remuneration for public employees was widely acknowledged to be inadequate, to be supplemented from other income-earning arrangements. Even before the official announcement of new regulations requiring greater self-reliance, local service delivery units were expected to look to their own resources to top-up official salaries, recouping the cost from consumers of services or running businesses on the side (Lam and Perry 2001; Painter 2006). In China, professional employees have been permitted under state regulations to provide fee-paying services to clients while in their official positions. Autonomisation was in many ways simply a formalisation of what was already happening "off-budget."

Subsequently, the service sector in becoming marketised has created an important set of economic interests in both China and Vietnam. Its capacity to extract fees and charges from households has created expanding business opportunities for a range of industries, from pharmaceuticals to textbook publishing. In the health sector, for example, opportunities for collusive practices (such as over-prescribing by doctors and use of public hospital facilities to set up for-profit ventures using high-tech medical equipment) have provided burgeoning opportunities for profit and for rent-seeking. For example, practices such as informal payments to doctors, over-prescribing and over-use of expensive clinical tests and equipment have been well documented in Vietnam and are in part the result of incentives built into the mixed public/private systems of funding, regulation and provision (Vasavakul 2009).

Governance and Service Delivery: Ideal and Reality

For Allen Schick and others, this headlong rush into service delivery marketisation would have rung alarm bells. Public sector discipline and accountability mechanisms of the kind familiar in highly institutionalised bureaucracies should have been implemented first, before embarking on autonomisation and deregulation; regulation of fees and charges and other budgetary control systems should have been put in place before giving service delivery agencies more discretion; and increasing the flexibility of employment terms and conditions without first enforcing those that already existed was a recipe for a range of abuses. As Schick argues, getting the formal bureaucratic rules and norms in place would seem to be the place to start, rather than giving delivery agencies more autonomy to operate in a commercial manner. If contracts or performance standards for public services were to be implemented in this new devolved system, enforceable rules and norms that would encourage compliance would first need to be in place. Instead, the commercialisation and autonomisation of public service delivery units increased the potential for various forms of "rent-seeking," abuse and corruption, resulting in growing dissatisfaction with many public services. For example, public hospitals have come in for some of the worst criticism on grounds of quality, affordability and profiteering (for example, over-prescribing of fake drugs at exorbitant monopoly prices) (Tam 2010).

However, in mounting such a critique, the underlying logic behind the actual steps taken needs to be understood. Framing of the problems occurred in a quite specific transition context, guided both by pragmatic concerns and also by traditions and patterns of socialist thought. The material to be worked with included a set of inherited party and state bodies, staffed by regime supporters and dependents whose livelihoods were at stake. Down-sizing was imperative, but wholesale redundancies unacceptable. In Vietnam (as in China) public discourse about development in a "market economy with socialist characteristics" lent legitimacy to the semi-privatisation of public services such as education and health at the local level. As the Vietnamese state emerged from the command economy, a distinction was drawn between state management on the one hand and the production of goods and services on the other. The former was seen as akin to "control and steering" and properly the business of the party and the state, while the provision or production role was seen as commercial or technical, to be left to the market and to society. The distinction was applied with the same meaning and consequences to the autonomisation of SOEs and of service delivery agencies alike, as both were viewed as production units (GSC 2000c, 8). As against the traditional style of "begging and giving" (or state subsidy), party leaders urged that enterprises and (in the same breath) public service delivery agencies should seek to mobilise "people's resources" in the form of a surplus derived from user fees and charges (GSC 2000a, 15). The term adopted was "socialisation," which was given specific local meaning and distinguished from the world-wide "privatisation" trend: "Socialization will be conducted under the principle the 'the work is shared between the State and the people,' and the State will take the principal role, exercising State management functions..." (GSC 2000b, 18).

To sum up, quasi-marketisation of service production and delivery was partly a matter of pragmatic convenience and partly a logical extension of the wider market reform agenda. What were missing from this agenda were the "good governance" building blocks, for example, the need for "due process" and other public-regarding rules and norms of the kind embodied in the routines of Weberian-style bureaucracies. Access and equity questions of the kind inherent in applying a concept of public goods were also side-lined, as were basic "consumer protection" provisions of the kind that pro-competitive, market-based service delivery reform would ideally include.[2] The answers to the fundamental problem of expanding production while unburdening the state payroll lay in new forms of self-sufficiency in a market context and in more flexible management arrangements, within a lightly regulated environment so as not to restrain local initiative and enterprise.

Retro-Fitting Better Governance

As already intimated, a by-product of these reforms has been to encourage service delivery abuses, including widespread corruption, and highly unequal access due both to affordability issues and also to the commercially-driven incentives driving investment in and location of facilities. Reliance on market mechanisms and user charges meant that poorer regions and groups missed out. A number of forces and interests have put pressure on the governments of China and Vietnam to change course. First, citizens have articulated high levels of dissatisfaction with both the growing burden of providing for rising education and health costs out of household income and also the low quality of some of these services. Associated corruption has also been a cause of complaint. Pressure to improve services and to ease access has been strongly felt by local officials. This dissatisfaction has created challenges to the party's legitimacy, which relies in large part on its continuing ability to deliver economic prosperity and social stability. Second, making provision for meeting the costs of health and education (in addition to housing, which has also been increasingly marketised) has come to be seen by the national government as a brake on economic development. High levels of savings are seen as an impediment to the growth of a more consumption-oriented middle class, which is seen as a future engine of growth for domestic industry. Improvements in public safety nets and public services are viewed in part as a measure to improve China's future growth prospects.

Remedial measures to cope with some of the adverse social and political consequences have begun to be taken by the Chinese and Vietnamese governments. In part, these measures reflect a shift in the balance of ongoing policy debates, with those arguing for a stronger role for the state in public goods provision gaining ground. More pertinently, they reflect a perception that the growing public dissatisfaction with the rising household costs of providing for housing, education and health (as well as the poor quality of many services) may threaten the future "performance legitimacy" of the ruling party. Three types of responses deserve brief mention: first, measures to deal with accountability issues at the "grass-roots" level; second, efforts to address some of the "market failures" of the privatised systems through regulatory reforms; and third, measures to restructure the finances of central and local governments so as to provide more budget support for public goods provision in poor localities.

On the accountability front, in both Vietnam and China, pre-existing citizen complaint mechanisms have been strengthened, albeit largely in forms that are consistent with exiting mechanisms for party management of dissent. This may enhance the capacity of party inspectorates and other disciplinary agencies to monitor and check abuses by local officials, while also affording local victims a safety valve for their grievances. In the case of "grass-roots democracy," in Vietnam new measures were introduced in the late 1990s in response to serious local unrest over local abuses of power and corruption. In both China and Vietnam, however, the capacity freely to choose local assemblies at village or commune level is constrained by mechanisms that monitor the nomination process, and uptake and implementation has been uneven from locality to locality (Levy 2003; Zingerli 2004). Moreover, the elected representatives are closely monitored and integrated into existing administrative hierarchies. In China, experiments with township elections were abruptly curtailed. In other words, these experiments in new accountability and "voice" mechanisms have sought primarily to contain and to deflect protest, without necessarily transforming the party's control over political mobilisation and interest articulation. By and large, despite some superficial similarities (*exempli gratia*, the adoption of so-called "citizen charters") these accountability mechanisms do not follow Western good governance models or practices.

With respect to directly addressing service delivery market failures and improving funding to local governments, the central government in China has begun to articulate a set of principles about the "welfare" role of government in assuring certain basic minimum standards and redressing inequalities. This is accompanied by new rhetoric about the "harmonious society," which deliberately echoes paternalistic Confucian doctrines. Modifications have occurred both in the ideological discourse and also in policy statements and outputs. Higher levels of financial support for the provision of infrastructure have been afforded to rural local governments and those in the western provinces; tougher regulation of fees and charges has been brought in; and there have been curbs on some forms of further privatisation. "Basic safety net" social insurance has been instituted to help overcome the exposure of citizens to the health services marketplace. With these measures, the pace of privatisation may be slowed while the state's role as basic provider, as well as regulator and guarantor, is being reassessed (Mok and Painter 2010).

Service delivery reforms in this context are in a state of flux. We may expect reforms to continue to be, by and large, incremental and reactive, particularly in the context of the strategic nature of political relations between central and local governments. In China's rural areas, some local experiments in commercialisation took place at first in a context of financial pressures following the clamp-down on local government fees and charges after 2003. Some local authorities went bankrupt and schools closed as a consequence of these rural tax reforms (Li 2007). Subsequently, central budget support and the shifting of service responsibilities to higher levels has been the preferred response, rather than yet more widespread autonomisation and devolution (Li 2008, 272). The official rhetoric is now focused more on fulfilling state responsibilities and on ensuring the equitable provision of basic public goods such as elementary education. While fees and charges remain a significant and indispensable element in the funding of such services, by the late 2000s these were more strictly regulated by higher levels of government, as were matters of service quality (Li 2008). The main elements in the reform agenda were increased financial transfers to local governments; assurances about guaranteed levels of funding; and measures to try to ensure local government compliance with central policies. Moreover, some recent evidence from the education sector suggests that local government officials have welcomed the new measures as offering them the means to fulfil their public service responsibilities, rather than (as critics might have expected) just pocketing the proceeds (Li 2011). In sum, reform is now arguably "back on track" in addressing core welfare and service quality issues.

Conclusion

Both in China and Vietnam, a commonly expressed metaphor to describe the style of reform in the transition era is: "crossing the river by feeling the stones." The unfolding of public service delivery reforms in China and Vietnam has been about resolving dilemmas associated with the transition from the command economy, one by one and step by step. The state was downsizing in numbers and withdrawing from micro-control, but expanding in policy reach. An emerging "middle class" demanded access to higher quality services and in order to meet this demand autonomisation and commercialisation were encouraged because public finances were inadequate for the task. This also in some measure solved the problem of how to pay public payroll wages and meet other costs. These developments suited local elites and gave new opportunities for patronage and profit. A distinctive socialist rhetoric of transition – "socialisation" and "self-sufficiency" – was used to justify the reforms. The "bad governance" consequences – to the extent that they have been recognised – were viewed by and large as a cost to be borne for the sake of expanding service production to serve both economic development and rising social expectations.

Most Western commentators on the progress of the Chinese and Vietnamese reforms have voiced a common set of criticisms of this experience, many of which can be summed up under the heading of "poor sequencing" (echoing the Allen Schick critique): autonomisation and commercialisation were encouraged before basic regulatory frameworks and policy coordination mechanisms were put in place; local personnel management was deregulated before a clear set of "reformed" public employment laws and regulations instilling basic civil service norms were instituted; local financial management experiments were initiated as a poor substitute for enhanced general revenue-raising capacity and before accounting controls and effective financial auditing were implemented; regulation and coordination of service access, affordability and quality were left for later, leading inexorably to service deficiencies; and so on.

Meanwhile, civil service reform, strengthening of legality and developing a service culture (all, according to good governance orthodoxy, necessary building blocks) have proceeded along different tracks at a much slower pace, constrained by politics and other circumstances. It is possible that some of these other reform agendas will also now gain more attention and receive more urgency. As markets in health and education have developed in order to boost production, the detrimental effects have given some producers and most consumers a financial interest in better regulation and more effective public accountability. Angry purchasers of expensive, fake drugs and worthless college degrees demand measures to stamp out corruption and regulate standards, while purveyors of higher quality products (such as the elite universities) want to restore the public's faith in their industry through similar reforms. In China and Vietnam, the entanglement of the service provision industries with local government and the prevalence of corruption and rent-seeking in these sectors means that the pressures for reform are meanwhile largely absorbed by the state. A range of legal, regulatory and financial rules are now being retrofitted: Chinese and Vietnamese governments are responding to market failures and political pressures in the health and education sectors by clarifying rules of subsidy, increasing transfer expenditures and better regulating the charging of fees and the provision of services. These measures might be expected to be accompanied by heightened levels of legality, accountability and transparency. In sum, good governance can come later.

Notes

[1] The distinction between "extra-budget" and "off-budget" funds is that the former are permitted under financial rules, the latter are not.

[2] A World Bank report on public service unit reform in China includes a chapter on state financing and organisation of public service provision in the West, trying to drive home the "lesson" that the public sector has a role in some "core" service provision functions (World Bank 2005a, 19–21). Cheng Siwei (2001), writing as a party intellectual and vice-chairman of the Standing Committee of the National People's

Congress, also criticizes reform efforts for not drawing upon a clear conception of "public goods" or the proper role of government in their provision.

References

Andrews, M. 2010. "Good Government Means Different Things in Different Countries." *Governance* 23 (1): 7–35.

Benewick, R., I. Tong, and J. Howell. 2004. "Self-Governance and Community: A Preliminary Comparison Between Villagers' Committees and Urban Community Councils." *China Information* 18 (1): 11–28.

Beresford, M. 2001. "Vietnam, the Transition From Central Planning." In *The Political Economy of South-East Asia*, 2nd ed. edited by G. Rodan, K. Hewison and R. Robison, 197–220. Melbourne: Oxford University Press.

Bernstein, T. P., and X. B. Lu. 2003. *Taxation Without Representation in Contemporary Rural China.* Cambridge: Cambridge University Press.

Brinkerhoff, D., and A. Goldsmith. 2005. "Institutional Dualism and International Development: A Revisionist Interpretation of Good Governance." *Administration and Society* 37 (2): 199–224.

Broadman, H. 2001. "The Business(Es) of the Chinese State." *The World Economy* 24 (7): 849–875.

Burns, J. 2001. "Public Sector Reform and the State: The Case of China." *Public Administration Quarterly* 24 (4): 419–436.

Carothers, T. 2007. "The 'Sequencing' Fallacy." *Journal of Democracy* 18 (1): 12–27.

Chan, H. 2004. "Cadre Personnel Management in China: The Nomenklatura System, 1990–1998." *The China Quarterly* 179: 703–734.

Cheng, S. 2001. "Strategic Directions and Policy Implementation for Reforming China's Institutional Units." In *Studies on Economic Reforms and Development in China*, edited by S. Cheng, 319–346. Oxford: Oxford University Press.

Dong, L., T. Christensen, and M. Painter. 2010a. "A Case Study of China's Administrative Reform – the Importation of the Super-Department." *American Review of Public Administration* 40 (2): 170–188.

Dong, L., T. Christensen, and M. Painter. 2010b. "Housing Reform in China: Rational Interests Gone Wrong or Organizational Design Failure?" *Journal of Asian Public Policy* 3 (1): 4–17.

Duckett, J. 1998. *The Entrepeneurial State in China: Real Estate and Commerce Departments in Reform Era Tianjin.* London: Routledge.

Duckett, J. 2001. "Bureaucrats in Business, China-Style: The Lessons of Market Reform and State Entrepreneurialism in the People's Republic of China." *World Development* 29 (1): 23–37.

Fforde, A. 1993. "The Political Economy of 'Reform' in Vietnam – Some Reflections." In *The Challenge of Reform in Indochina*, edited by B. Ljunggren, 293–326. Cambridge: Harvard Institute for International Development, Harvard University.

Fforde, A. 2005. "State-Owned Enterprises, Law and a Decade of Market-Oriented Socialist Development in Vietnam." In *Asian Socialism and Legal Change, the Dynamics of Vietnamese and Chinese Reform*, edited by J. Gillespie and P. Nicholson, 239–266. Canberra: Asia Pacific Press.

Foster, K. 2005. "Chinese Public Policy Innovation and the Diffusion of Innovations: An Initial Exploration." *Chinese Public Administration Review* 3 (1): 1–13.

Gainsborough, M. 2003. *Changing Political Economy of Vietnam: The Case of Ho Chi Minh City.* London: Routledge Curzon.

Gillespie, J. 2002. "The Political-Legal Culture of Anti-Corruption Reforms in China." In *Corruption in Asia: Rethinking the Governance Paradigm*, edited by T. Lindsey and H. Dick, 167–200. Sydney: The Federation Press.

Gillespie, J. 2005. "Changing Concepts of Socialist Law in Vietnam." In *Asian Socialism and Legal Change, the Dynamics of Vietnamese and Chinese Reform*, edited by J. Gillespie and P. Nicholson, 45–76. Canberra: Asia Pacific Press.

Gillespie, J. 2006. *Transplanting Commercial Law Reform: Developing a 'Rule of Law' in Vietnam.* Aldershot: Ashgate.

Goldsmith, A. 2007. "Is Governance Reform a Catalyst for Development?" *Governance* 20 (2): 165–186.

Gong, T. 2006. "Corruption and Local Governance: The Double Identity of Chinese Local Governments in Market Reform." *The Pacific Review* 19 (1): 85–102.

Gong, T. 2008. "The Party Discipline Inspection in China: Its Evolving Trajectory and Embedded Dilemmas." *Crime, Law and Social Change* 49 (2): 139–152.

Grindle, M. 2004. "Good Enough Governance: Poverty Reduction and Reform in Developing Countries." *Governance* 17 (4): 525–548.

GSC (Government Steering Committee for Public Administration Reform). 2000a. *The Overall Report: Review of Public Administration Reform.* Hanoi: Government of Vietnam.

GSC. 2000b. *Report of Group 1: Stances and Guidelines of the Party and the Sate of Vietnam on Public Administration Reform.* Hanoi: Government of Vietnam.

GSC. 2000c. *Report of Group 3: Review of Public Administration Reform in the Field of Organizational Structure of the Government Apparatus and State Management – Roles, Functions, Responsibilities and Structure.* Hanoi: Government of Vietnam.

Gu, E., and J. Zhang. 2006. "Health Care Regime Change in Urban China: Unmanaged Marketization and Reluctant Privatization." *Pacific Affairs* 79 (1): 49–71.

Holmberg, S., B. Rothstein, and N. Nasiritousi. 2008. "Quality of Government: What You Get." Gothenburg: Quality of Government Institute, University of Gothenburg, QOG Working Paper Series 2008, 21.

Khan, M. 2007. "Governance, Economic Growth and Development since the 1960s." United Nations, DESA Working Paper No. 54.

Lam, T., and J. Perry. 2001. "Service Organizations in China: Reform and Its Limits." In *Remaking China's Public Management,* edited by N. Lee, and W. Lo, 19–40. Westport: Quorum Books.

Levy, R. 2003. "The Village Self-Government Movement: Elections, Democracy, the Party and Anticorruption – Developments in Guangdong." *China Information* 17 (1): 28–65.

Li, L. 2002. "The Politics of Introducing Direct Township Elections in China." *The China Quarterly* 171: 704–723.

Li, L. 2007. "Working for the Peasants? – Strategic Interactions and Unintended Consequences in the Chinese Rural Tax Reform." *China Journal* 57: 89–106.

Li, L. 2008. "State and Market in Public Service Provision: Opportunities and Traps for Institutional Change in Rural China." *The Pacific Review* 21 (3): 257–278.

Li, L. 2011. "Strategic Action and Local Fiscal Policy: How Cadres Manage Scarcity – or Abundance?" Paper presented at the International Workshop on Politics and Autonomy in China's Local State – County and Township Cadres as Strategic Groups, Tubingen University, Germany, July 1–3.

London, J. 2006. "The Political Economy of Education in a 'Socialist' Periphery." *Asia Pacific Journal of Education* 26 (1): 1–20.

Lu, X. 2000. "Booty Socialism, Bureau-Preneurs and the State in Transition: Organizational Corruption in China." *Comparative Politics* 32 (3): 273–294.

Mok, K., and M. Painter. 2010. "Reasserting the Public in Public Service Delivery: The De-Privatization and De-Marketization of Education in China." In *Reasserting the State in Public Services,* edited by M. Ramesh, E. Araral, and X. Wu, 137–158. London: Routledge.

Mountfield, E., and C. Wong. 2005. "Public Expenditure on the Frontline: Toward Effective Management by Subnational Governments." In *East Asia Decentralizes: Making Local Government Work,* edited by World Bank, 85–106. Washington, DC: World Bank.

Ngok, K., and H. Chan. 2003. "Guest Editors' Introduction." *Chinese Law and Government* 36 (1): 5–13.

Oi, J. C. 1999. *Rural China Takes Off: Institutional Foundations of Economic Reform.* Berkeley: University of California Press.

Oi, J. C., and S. Rozelle. 2000. "Elections and Power: The Locus of Decision-Making in Chinese Villages." *The China Quarterly* 162: 513–539.

Painter, M. 2002. "Making Sense of Good Governance." *Public Administration and Policy* 11 (2): 77–100.

Painter, M. 2003. "Public Administration Reform in Vietnam: Problems and Prospects." *Public Administration and Development* 23: 259–271.

Painter, M. 2006. "Sequencing Civil Service Pay Reforms in Vietnam: Transition or Leapfrog?" *Governance* 19 (2): 325–348.

Peerenboom, R., ed. 2004. *Asian Discourses of Rule of Law: Theories and Implementation of Rule of Law in Twelve Asian Countries, France and the US.* London: Routledge Curzon.

Peerenboom, R. 2009. "Rule of Law, Democracy and the Sequencing Debate: Lessons from China and Vietnam." Accessed on 12 August 2011. http://ssrn.com/abstract=1447051.

Schick, A. 1998. "Why Most Developing Countries Should Not Try New Zealand Reforms." *The World Bank Research Observer* 13: 1123–1131.

Shirk, S. 1992. "The Chinese Political System and the Political Strategy of Economic Reform." In *Bureaucrats, Politics and Decision Making in Post-Mao China*, edited by K. Liberthal, and D. Lampton, 59–91. Berkeley: University of California Press.

Tam, W. 2010. "Privatising Healthcare in China: Problems and Reforms." *Journal of Contemporary Asia* 40 (1): 63–81.

Tandberg, E., and M. Pavesic-Skerlep. 2009. "Advanced Public Financial Management Reforms in South East Europe." International Monetary Fund, Working Paper, WP/09/102.

Vasavakul, T. 2009. *Corruption in the Health Sector: Management of Service Delivery and Impact on Poverty Reduction in Vietnam*. Hanoi: Embassy of Sweden.

Wallsten, S. 2002. "Does Sequencing Matter? Regulation and Privatization in Telecommunications Reforms." Work Bank, Development Research Group, Policy Research Working Paper 2817.

Wedeman, A. 2000. "Budgets, Extra-Budgets and Small Treasuries." *Journal of Contemporary China* 9: 489–511.

Wong, L., and J. Tang. 2006. "Non-State Care Homes for Older People as Third Sector Organizations in China's Transitional Welfare Economy." *Journal of Social Policy* 35 (2): 229–246.

World Bank. 1994. *Governance: The World Bank's Experience*. Washington, DC: World Bank.

World Bank. 2003. *World Development Report 2004: Making Services Work for Poor People*. Washington DC: World Bank.

World Bank. 2005a. *Report No. 32341-CHA: China Deepening Public Service Unit Reform to Improve Service Delivery*. Washington, DC: World Bank.

World Bank. 2005b. *Vietnam, Managing Public Expenditure for Poverty Reduction and Growth – Public Expenditure Review and Integrated Fiduciary Assessment (Volume 1: Cross Sectoral Issues)*. Washington, DC; World Bank.

Yang, D. 2004. *Remaking the Chinese Leviathan. Market Transition and the Politics of Governance in China*. Stanford: Stanford University Press.

Zingerli, C. 2004. "Politics in Mountain Communes: Exploring Vietnamese Grassroots Democracy." In *Rethinking Vietnam*, edited by D. McCargo, 53–66. London: Routledge Curzon.

The Heterodoxy of Governance under Decentralisation: Rent-Seeking Politics in China's Tobacco Growing Areas

YI-WEN CHENG* & TAK-WING NGO**

*Leiden Institute of Area Studies, Leiden University, Leiden, The Netherlands, **Department of Government and Public Administration, University of Macau, Taipa, Macau, China

ABSTRACT *This paper questions the categorisation of good/bad governance and argues that such a stylised conception fails to capture the ambivalence of responsibilities and accountabilities in a political system characterised by multiple layers of authorities. Using a case study of the tobacco monopoly in China, the paper shows the contradictory goals and outcomes in different modes of operation that defy a stylised categorisation. A vigorously enforced regulatory regime with a higher level of transparency and bureaucratic accountability raised the national revenue and put tobacco production in accordance with the national plan. Yet it has severely impaired the welfare and livelihood of tobacco peasants. Conversely, a regulatory regime captured by parochial interests and sabotaged by rent-seeking politics rendered bureaucratic authority arbitrary and opaque, and at the expense of the state plan and national interests. Nonetheless it protected the welfare of peasants, improved local production and helped develop the local economy. The paper argues that the pathways to good governance are not only multi-linear, but also heterodox and unpredictable.*

The normative concept of good governance represents to a large extent an assortment of characteristics deriving from the historical experience of Western countries. These characteristics include such institutional, procedural and performance indicators of managing public affairs as being participatory, consensus-oriented, accountable, transparent, responsive, effective and efficient, equitable and inclusive and following the rule of law. While admitting that few countries have achieved good governance in its totality, advocates argue that this remains a workable ideal. Bad governance is still seen as the root cause of major social problems in the developing world.

Such a stylised conception of governance has been rightly criticised by many observers. A number of revisionist attempts have redefined the concept to make it more analytically useful and practically more viable as a guide to development. Some researchers have conceptualised good/bad governance along a continuum, and prefer to talk about "governance quality" or "governance performance" (Hyden, Court, and Mease 2004). Others have pointed out that the baggage of good governance contains virtually all aspects of public administration from institutional rules to decision-making to resource management. In this sense, achieving good governance is not far from asking for a radical change in the social, economic and political system. To make the task less overwhelming for developing countries, some advocate the idea of "good enough governance" which focuses on narrower, and hence more manageable, aspects of institutional improvement such as those relating to poverty reduction (Grindle 2004). Still others have pointed out that there are multiple pathways to good governance. The historical differences between Asian, African and Latin American countries will oblige different countries to chart their own course of action.

However, even these revisionist ideas of good governance are not lacking in ambiguities and contradictions. Such ambiguities include, most notably, the assumptions that improvements in different dimensions of governance are mutually compatible, that good institutions and procedures will bring about desirable social and developmental outcomes, and that the culmination of incremental progress in different governance institutions will result in good enough governance. Whilst these assumptions may sound logical, the actual development often ends up otherwise. This is particularly so when the idea of good (enough) governance is presented as a packaged recipe. The desirable elements such as political accountability, administrative transparency, policy effectiveness, social inclusion, rule of law, and so on, are supposed to work together and reinforce one another in the package. The prescribed package is considered to be "good" by definitional fiat, without making reference to the actual outcomes, both intended and unintended.

We argue here that conceptualising good governance in terms of a prescribed package of institutional and procedural setups fails to capture the complexity and the dilemmatic nature of governance, especially in those polities characterised by multiple layers of authorities. In particular, the discrepancies between seemingly "good" institutional practices at the national level and the actual outcomes at the grass-roots level can be substantial. Our hypothesis is that governance will be effective only when there is congruence between the goals of decentralised administration and the objectives of national reforms. Where this is absent, governance will be at best heterodox and unpredictable.

Bringing the Local Back into the Heterodoxy of Governance

From the outset, different elements in a good governance package may contradict each other. For instance, studies on East Asian governance have long identified social exclusion and insulated technocratic autonomy as the basis of state capacity in effecting developmental plans (Johnson 1982; Evans 1995). Here bureaucratic transparency, social inclusion and participatory politics do not go hand in hand with state-led development, administrative efficiency and policy efficacy. Furthermore, the emphasis on institutional and procedural arrangements as bases of good governance overlooks the broader historical, social and political contexts within which institutions work – that is, governance institutions are fashioned by social structures in their operation and function (Waldner 1999; Chibber 2003). Similar institutional setups may therefore produce dissimilar outcomes in different countries (Ngo 2006). Institutions that produce "good" outcomes in one case can end up in "bad" governance in another. The most common example can be found in democratising regimes in ethnically divided societies. The introduction of electoral politics often leads to extreme social polarisation and partisan competition. Instead of serving as a means of enhancing social inclusion, political legitimacy and governmental accountability, electoral politics may become an instrument of group domination and exclusion. This is well-documented in comparative studies of developmental experiences, even in exemplary cases of successful democratic transition (Mattlin 2011; Ngo 2004).

There is one further complication in the good governance formula. Until recently, much of the attention has been focused on the nation-wide institutions. Governance at the national level has often been assumed, or taken for granted, to be more important than local governance. Yet there is growing evidence that governance outcomes are not only shaped by national institutions but also influenced by local circumstances. Sub-national governance has gained increasing importance under decentralisation in many countries. The presence of local governance further contributes to the contradiction and heterodoxy of the good governance package.

To begin with, the devolution of state power enables local authorities to direct their attention and resources to turning their sub-national territorial units into sources of growth and competition. The process represents a kind of state re-scaling, to borrow Brenner's idea (1998), through which local states reconfigure themselves as an institutional, regulatory and territorial precondition to serve the sub-national geographies of accelerated accumulation. It is believed that decentralisation promotes good governance by enabling citizen participation and enhancing social responsiveness. However, in this exercise, the governance of sub-national units assumes its own goals, procedures and means vis-à-vis national governance. It is not difficult to locate contradictions and tensions between local and national governance.

The contradictions and tensions under decentralised governance can be fully demonstrated in our case study of China. Since the introduction of the market reform three decades ago, numerous administrative and institutional reforms have been implemented by the Chinese government. Although the regime still falls short of a system characterised by democracy and the rule of law, serious efforts have been undertaken to improve administrative accountability, bureaucratic transparency, professionalisation of the civil service and so on (Yang 2004). While the Chinese system cannot be seen as an example of good governance, over the years China has undeniably been striving for "better" governance.

Such improvement in governance has been accompanied by extensive decentralisation. It includes the major forms of decentralisation in terms of deconcentration, devolution and delegation (Cheema and Rondinelli 2007). To begin with, regulatory and supervisory powers have been granted to regional bureaux of national ministries and departments in administering local affairs. At the same time, local governments have been given extensive fiscal and administrative power to meet the needs of their local population. In return, they are required to balance their own budget, promote local economic growth, sustain a high rate of employment, ensure social stability and fulfil the tasks handed down by higher levels of government. Under a contract system, the responsibilities of each local government are set out in great detail against which the performance of leading local cadres is assessed (Edin 2000; Whiting 2000; Gao 2009). Local cadres are therefore held accountable for what they have achieved or failed to do in the region under their jurisdiction. Finally, managerial functions have been delegated to state enterprises and parastatal organisations to carry out specific tasks.

Advocates of decentralised governance believe that decentralisation can bring about more effective governance. However, empirical studies have found that the outcomes of decentralised governance are uneven, and evidence of a direct relationship between decentralisation and developmental progress is anything but strong (Davoodi and Zou 1998; Martinez-Vazquez and McNab 2003). In a recent study of 30 Mexican municipalities, Grindle (2009) finds that decentralisation leads to better local governance in some cases but not in others. The same situation can be found in the case of the Philippines after two decades of decentralisation (Lange 2010). The improvement in democracy and local services is anything but uniform. While decentralisation facilitates policy reforms quickly, the sustainability of those changes is often undermined by institutional weaknesses. Likewise, citizen participation is more effective in extracting resources than in holding local agencies accountable.

In the case of China, the outcome is at best controversial (Dirlik 2012). The devolution of state power enables local authorities to direct their attention and resources to turning their sub-national territorial units into a source of growth and competition. The immediate outcome is severe competition between localities, both in terms of actual benefits, such as access to resources and investments, as well as symbolic achievements such as higher ranking in competitiveness. Existing scholarship differs in its assessment of the consequences of such competition. Montinola, Qian, and Weingast (1995) argue that inter-regional competition constitutes a kind of Chinese-style federalism and is the source of China's rapid growth. In contrast, Pei (2006) suggests that it is a kind of predatory decentralisation which leads to local protectionism and widespread rent seeking.

The controversy and unevenness relating to decentralisation is in fact closely linked to the heterodoxy of governance. Just as advocates of good governance assume that different elements in a good governance package are mutually compatible, advocates of decentralisation tend to see deconcentration, devolution and delegation as complementary in nature. This cannot be farther from the truth. To use China as an example, deconcentration and devolution created separate sets of jurisdiction, control, accountability and interests. The vertical hierarchy of administrative responsibilities formed under deconcentration (usually referred to as *tiao*, literally meaning strips) often runs into conflict with local governments who gained extensive fiscal and administrative autonomy under devolution (usually referred to as *kuai*, literally meaning blocks). The result is a decentralised system characterised by multiple levels of administration across a vast number of regions. Bargaining and contention between sectional interests occur along vertical hierarchies of functional administration as well as across horizontal levels of territorial government. The crisscrossing of various jurisdictions constitutes a complicated power matrix known as the *tiao-kuai* system (Mertha 2005). The fragmentation of authority under such an administrative matrix generates conflicting goals and responsibilities.

In other words, the conflicting goals and responsibilities generated by different forms of decentralisation are mapped onto contradictory elements of the good governance package. For instance, social inclusion in a particular locality can become parochialism from a national perspective; while the accountability of local officials towards their supervisory authorities at the central level can be achieved at the expense of local responsiveness. As such, the discrepancies between good national institutions/practices and local outcomes can be substantial. Our hypothesis is that decentralised governance will be most effective in places where there is congruence between the goals of various decentralisation initiatives and the objectives of governance reforms. In most cases where such congruence is absent, local governments will be juggling with contradictory demands under multiple layers of authority. Our case study below will shed light on this argument.

Furthermore, since local governance is shaped by the nature of local politics, the congruence and incongruence between goals of decentralisation and governance objectives vary across regions. It follows that the quality of national governance will depend on the clashes and meshes between decentralised governance regimes at different sub-national levels. In other words, the conventional good governance package needs to be unpacked, since one may not be able to come up with a uniform, prescriptive package that suits all central and local situations even within a single country. This underlines the fact that the pathways to good governance are not only multi-linear, but also heterodox and at best unpredictable. The heterodoxy of governance stands in contrast to the conventional assumption about the possibility – and desirability – of striving for a uniform and coherent package of good governance composed of mutually compatible and reinforcing institutional and procedural setups. Instead, our conception highlights the potential incongruence between governing institutions across space and fields, and explores the conditions under which congruence or compromise is made possible.

Decentralised Governance and the Tobacco Monopoly in China

This paper examines the problems of decentralised governance in terms of conflicting demands and responsibilities by looking at the case of China. Specifically, we study the regions of Yunnan and Guizhou. These two provinces face a number of problems which are highly illustrative of the contradictions mentioned above. As the major tobacco growing areas in China, Yunnan and Guizhou have been closely linked to the tobacco economy in their governance. From the outset, China has a huge population of smokers. It is home to one-quarter of the world's smokers while one-third of the world's cigarettes are consumed in China. As the world's largest tobacco producer and consumer, revenue from tobacco constitutes a substantial proportion of the national income. From the state's point of view, effective management of the tobacco revenue is essential to the country's fiscal account. At the same time, under devolution, local governments in Yunnan and Guizhou have been motivated to get involved with the tobacco business because they too have been relying heavily on tobacco income as a source of revenue, given limited industrialisation and foreign investments in these regions.

Conflicts within the *tiao-kuai* arose when a state tobacco monopoly was established to maximise tax and revenue. In accordance with the thrust of deconcentration, the responsibilities of administering the cigarette production quota have been delegated down the line of hierarchy. Local state enterprises have been entrusted with the function of manufacturing cigarettes under the principle of delegation. In theory, local governments, state enterprises and local monopoly authorities have clear divisions of labour and jurisdiction. In practice, however, instead of becoming complementary partners in realising state goals, the interested parties either conspired to capture the monopolistic rent from the national treasury, or pursued their own interests at the expense of the others. Paradoxical outcomes can be seen during intra-bureaucratic contentions. When the tobacco monopoly was captured by parochial interests and sabotaged by rent-seeking politics, administrative accountability became arbitrary and opaque. Local benefits took precedence over state plans and national interests. Nonetheless, it protected the welfare of peasants, improved local production and helped develop the local economy. Conversely, when the regime of state monopoly was vigorously enforced, administrative transparency and bureaucratic accountability improved. The national revenue was effectively increased and production was pursued in accordance with the national plan. Yet such vigorous enforcement severely impaired the welfare and livelihood of tobacco peasants.

In the following, we will explain this paradox and identify the institutional logic behind such outcomes. To begin with, let us take a look at the tobacco monopoly. Set up in 1982, the national tobacco monopoly was established with a view to maximising revenue for the state purse. Under this regime, the state monopolised the production and sale of cigarettes, as well as the procurement of tobacco leaves from peasants. In other words, the entire production chain was put under the control of a state monopoly-cum-monopsony. Ironically, this runs against the national trend of economic liberalisation and increasing market competition.

The creation of the tobacco monopoly represented an attempt by the central government to regain control of a decentralised regime. The key concern of the central government was the mismatch between the supply of tobacco leaves and the production of cigarettes. Such a concern began as early as 1964, when Beijing created the Chinese Tobacco Industrial Corporation as a national trust to oversee and manage the entire tobacco industry. During the Cultural Revolution, the corporation was dissolved and its duties devolved to local authorities. As a result, local cigarette factories mushroomed under production brigades and teams. These local factories competed for raw materials with state-licensed factories, and forced the latter to reduce or stop production. Eventually, the State Council ordered a clamp down on local factories in 1977 (Yang 2009).

When market reform kicked off in the early 1980s, local governments were once again allowed and even encouraged to operate local cigarette factories. Before long, the proliferation of local cigarette manufacturers resulted in an acute shortage of tobacco leaves. Many state factories failed to reach their production targets. From the central government's point of view, this resulted in a transfer of revenue from the national income to the local purse. In response, the State Council set up the China National Tobacco Corporation (CNTC) as the main agent of centralised management for the tobacco industry in 1982. In the following year, the *Rules on the Tobacco Monopoly* were promulgated, hence formally institutionalising a state tobacco monopoly.

According to the rules, only the CNTC was allowed to buy tobacco leaves from farmers and to sell those leaves to cigarette factories. Factories could only engage in cigarette manufacture and were required to sell all their cigarette products back to the CNTC. This meant that China's tobacco system became a monopoly-cum-monopsony regime, with the CNTC as the only cigarette wholesaler to all licensed retailers as well as the sole buyer of tobacco leaves from growers.[1]

In the meantime, the State Tobacco Monopoly Administration (STMA) was set up in accordance with the provisions of the rules. The STMA was responsible for formulating developmental strategies for the tobacco industry, enforcing regulations related to the tobacco monopoly, handling cases of violation and so on. In essence, the STMA was responsible for enforcing the annual quota of cigarette production while the CNTC was engaging in the actual tobacco trade. However, the division of labour between the CNTC and the STMA was anything but clear. In practice they shared the same set of personnel within a unified line of command – a common form of organisational setup in China known as "one crew with two separate titles" (*liang kuai paizi, yi tao renma* 兩塊牌子，一套人馬).

The tobacco monopoly reminds us of the command economy before market reform. The CNTC and the STMA carried out their activities on behalf of the state. Through their local corporations/agencies in provinces, cities and counties, the CNTC and the STMA were obliged to observe the plans laid down by the central planning authorities.[2] Annual plans for tobacco leaf plantation, procurement, leaf quality grades and cigarette production quotas were formulated and issued to the CNTC and all cigarette factories to follow.

The tobacco monopoly is criticised for being "the last fortress of the planned economy" in China. It may appear to be an extreme case of a counter-liberalisation move. However, similar moves can in fact be found in a number of sectors in China, such as electricity, telecommunications and the railway, although their degree of concentration is less extreme (Irwin Crookes 2012). Even in consumer commodities such as cotton, studies have found that the transition from state-controlled supply and marketing cooperatives to a cotton market has met with counter-liberalisation efforts from local governments to retain control of the cotton trade (Alpermann 2010).

Despite the progress in economic reform during the 1980s and the early 1990s, much of the tobacco regime has remained unscathed. Some minor changes were made when the rules were replaced by the *Tobacco Monopoly Law* in 1992, but in general the regulatory regime remained more or less the same. The operation of the tobacco monopoly has aroused heated debates. Critics were sceptical about the policy since it ran counter to the idea of market reform. However, concern about fiscal stability at the time overrode the market argument. Under fiscal decentralisation, the consolidated government budget as a share of national income shrank from an average of 38% in the late 1970s to 24% by 1988–89 (Wong 1991). The central leadership was alarmed by the fiscal decline. At this juncture, income generated from the tobacco industry contributed significantly to state revenue, as Table 1 shows. Because of that, the state treasury was unwilling to lose this stable source of income.

Table 1. Ratio of tobacco income in national revenue (1976–2007)

Period/year	Tobacco income[a] (RMB, hundred million)	National revenue (RMB, hundred million)	TI to NR ratio (%)
Fifth five-year plan period (1976–80)	200.24	4,960.66	4.04
Sixth five-year plan period (1981–85)	377.07	6,830.68	5.52
Seventh five-year plan period (1986–90)	1065	13,421.16	7.93
Eighth five-year plan period (1991–95)	2,261	24,256.08	9.32
1996	830	7,408	11.2
1997	900	8,651.1	10.4
1998	950	9,876	9.6
1999	989	11,444.1	8.6
2000	1,050	13,380.1	7.8
2001	1,150	16,371	7.0
2002	1,400	18,914	7.4
2003	1,600	21715.3	7.4
2004	2,100	25,178	8.3
2005	2,400	31,649.29	7.6
2006	2,900	39,373.2	7.4
2007	3,880	51,304.03	7.6

Notes: [a]Tobacco income includes the tax and profit.
Source: STMA and National Bureau of Statistics of China, cited in Wang (2009, 23).

Local Adaptation of the Tobacco Monopsony

In order to maximise and stabilise the revenue, the government sought to ensure that the whole tobacco sector worked according to a national plan. In principle, the State Planning Commission would issue a tobacco procurement plan every year. Based on this plan, county tobacco corporations would, through their local agencies, sign procurement contracts with tobacco growers. The contract would specify the planting area and production quantity, as well as subsidies for seeds and fertilisers used in the cultivation. After flue-curing, tobacco growers were required to sell their outputs to the CNTC at fixed prices. In this transaction, tobacco growers had little choice but to sell their tobacco leaves to the CNTC as the sole purchaser. The monopsony thus guaranteed that the central procurement plan would be implemented according to set criteria.[3] The whole system was designed to match production demand and agricultural supply under a national plan. There was little consideration of local variations. The situation of individual tobacco peasants or local tobacco corporations had no role in the plan. Social responsiveness was not part of the governance formula.

In practice, however, the operation of tobacco procurement worked otherwise. It was shaped by the institutional dynamics under decentralisation. Although the CNTC was the sole purchaser by regulation, actual business operation was controlled by its local agents, which was strongly influenced by local governments. Under deconcentration, the CNTC managed its local agencies mainly through personnel appointment. At each level of the administrative hierarchy – the *tiao* – a superior tobacco corporation would supervise its subordinates. However, tobacco corporations at each administrative level retained their own budgetary account, and enjoyed the autonomy of handling their corporate assets. In other words, under such deconcentration, a high degree of fiscal autonomy was enjoyed by local tobacco corporations at least until 2005. Figure 1 illustrates such a relationship.

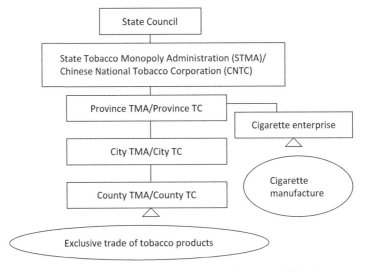

Figure 1. Structural organisation of the tobacco monopoly*. *Notes*: *The figure presents the structure of the tobacco monopoly system before 2003, when the structural reform was initiated. After that, in 2004, the corporate capacity of the county tobacco corporation was cancelled, and hence the county level was no longer allowed to run a tobacco business.

The administration of local corporations under the *tiao* hierarchy was complicated by the jurisdiction of the *kuai* under devolution. With enlarged authorities and autonomies of local governments, any major personnel change in a local tobacco corporation would in fact require the approval of the respective local government. The arrangement gave local governments a certain leverage in the tobacco regime. At the same time, local tobacco corporations also enjoyed a substantial degree of autonomy in the actual operation. The actual functioning of the tobacco monopsony at the practical level therefore depended very much on the collusion between local governments and local tobacco corporations.

Instead of fulfilling the national goal of matching demand and supply in an annual quota, local governments had their own objective: maximising local revenue. Local cadres were eager to tap into the potential revenue generated from the tobacco monopsony. Under fiscal and administrative decentralisation, the more revenue local governments could collect, the more they could keep and spend on local development (Oi 1999). Such an imperative was reinforced by the cadre responsibility system. Under this system, leading cadres at a particular level of government have to sign a performance contract with the higher-level government. Their performance is then evaluated against the criteria set down in the contract. The assessment will affect not only the cadres' bonuses but also their promotion. Although some local variations in evaluation criteria exist, tax remittance almost always appears as one of the most important performance targets (Edin 2000; Whiting 2000).

The ability to generate sufficient local revenue is therefore a central concern for all local governments. Yet most local authorities at the lower and grass-roots levels have been struggling with the problem of insufficient income. This is because when fiscal responsibility was devolved to local governments, so were administrative responsibilities. Local governments were required not only to balance their own budgets, but also to provide social welfare and to fund infrastructural development. For example, county governments had to shoulder the expense of social security, and township governments had to provide compulsory education in rural areas. These expenses severely undermined the financial capacity of local governments, in particular for inland rural areas where the collapse of collectivised agriculture was not followed by rapid industrialisation (Wong and Bhattasali 2003; Wong 1991).The disparity between limited income and substantial expenditure obligations thus drove local governments to secure funding by whatever means available.

In such circumstances, the tax revenue from tobacco leaves played a significant role in major tobacco-producing areas, especially in the poor rural areas in western China where industrialisation had been slow and foreign investment very limited (Peng 1996). In these areas, local governments could collect a 38% special agricultural product tax – the highest rate among agricultural products – which was levied on all purchases of flue-cured tobacco leaves by local tobacco corporations from the peasants.[4] Because of that, it was tempting for local governments to encourage the harvest of tobacco leaves and the sale of these leaves to tobacco corporations.

Growing Outside the Plan

From the points above we can see the conflicting goals under decentralised governance. From the outset, the establishment of the tobacco monopsony was meant to deliver handsome economic rents to the state treasury. The CNTC and its local agents were supposedly the representatives of state interests in managing the system. Local governments were required to facilitate rent extraction, and in return they would be rewarded with the product tax which they could use for local development. But local governments were also required to look after their own budgets. They were thus inclined to manipulate the monopsony in order to capture part of the economic rent. In addition to local governments, local tobacco corporations, cigarette factories and tobacco peasants also colluded together to take advantage of the tobacco monopsony. Their actions constituted a form of local governance that was intricately linked to parochial interests. This eventually led to the subversion of the annual production quota.

To understand the emergence of such a form of governance and the rent-seeking politics involved, let us briefly look at the manipulations and actions of various economic actors in the tobacco growing areas. In the case of the cigarette factories, they could easily manipulate their production plan because of the fiscal autonomy granted to state-owned enterprises (SOEs) during the market reform. Under such autonomy, SOEs could produce beyond the annual quota assigned to them, and were allowed to sell their extra production in the market. Let us take the case of the Yuxi Cigarette Factory (the predecessor of the Hongta Tobacco Group) in Yunnan Province as an example. Although the sales rights of all within-plan cigarettes rested with the CNTC, Yuxi was allowed to sell 80% of its beyond-plan cigarettes. The profit derived from beyond-plan sales would be kept by Yuxi. It could be used to buy auxiliary materials for cigarette production such as rolling paper, filters and paper for packaging. This applied to the purchase of tobacco leaves as well.

In principle, the central government formulated an annual tobacco leaf cultivation target for peasants and a cigarette production target for SOEs. Yet cigarette factories could produce more than the quota as long as they obtained sufficient production materials, which in turn relied on the production of tobacco leaves beyond the quota (Interview with retired Hongta manager, September 7, 2009). As a result, this created a tobacco market outside the state plan. Through this market, cigarette factories could get extra tobacco leaves to supply their beyond-plan production, whereas local tobacco corporations could profit by selling the surplus tobacco leaves. As such, peasants were encouraged by local governments who wanted more tobacco tax to grow tobacco leaves above their contract quotas.

In fact, it was not only the local governments and tobacco corporations at the grass-roots level which benefited from this manipulation. Other governments and tobacco corporations in the higher *tiao-kuai* hierarchy also took advantage of such practice. In the case of Yunnan Province, during the Sixth Five-Year Plan (1981–85), taxation on within-plan tobacco leaves was retained locally, while taxation on beyond-plan tobacco leaves was shared with the superior authorities within the province. In other words, governments at different levels could benefit from the beyond-plan tobacco as well. In the case of tobacco corporations, county tobacco corporations could retain 70% of beyond-plan tobacco leaves, with the remaining 30% to be handed over to the provincial tobacco corporation. As such, county corporations could sell their surplus procurements to cigarette factories to increase their incomes. At the same time, municipal and provincial corporations would benefit from the remittances from the surplus procurements.[5] In Guizhou, some municipal and provincial tobacco corporations even charged an additional "administrative fee" against their county corporations for handling surplus procurements (Interview with Guizhou Tobacco Corporation staff, July 19, 2009).

Consequently, under income considerations of local stakeholders, the volume of tobacco products grew outside the plan. But there is one additional reason for such growth. Under the pressure of local governments, county tobacco corporations often purchased all the tobacco leaves cultivated by peasants, regardless of the amount specified in the contracts. This derived from the local government policy to avoid peasant unrest. Unlike other commercial crops, tobacco leaves can only be used for cigarette production. And under state monopsony, peasants had nowhere else to sell their crops. If the county tobacco corporations refused to buy over-produced tobacco leaves, the loss for the peasants would be severe. In order to prevent any peasant unrest, county tobacco corporations would go along with the local government's request to purchase all tobacco leaves. Over time this became the norm and a part of peasant welfare. Peasants expected that tobacco corporations would buy up their entire yield, regardless of the procurement quantity specified in the contract. As a result, the sales guarantee further encouraged peasants to raise their production, especially when the procurement price of tobacco leaves was higher than the price of staple crops.

Because of this situation, the national plan set by the state tobacco monopsony was severely undermined by local collusion. Due to the manipulation of various interested parties, the national plan for tobacco production existed only in name. The STMA was unable to keep tobacco cultivation and procurement under control. Instead, blind production was encouraged by local governments under the fiscal responsibility system. In balancing the conflict between local interests and the national plan, most local governments chose to protect the former.

Local Welfare under Decentralised Governance

By 1997, the situation became increasingly uncontrollable as overproduction threatened to undermine the entire state monopoly. The problem was aggravated by the change in central–local fiscal relations. The central government undertook radical fiscal reform in 1994 with the introduction of a tax-sharing system. Under this new system, all tax revenue was divided into three categories: central tax, local tax and shared tax. This allowed the central government to exact its revenue directly from the central tax rather than to rely on local remittance. The resulting change was remarkable: before the reform, tax distribution between the central and local governments was 22:78 in 1993, and under the new system it became 55.7:44.3 in 1994 (Yang and Yang 2008).

The diminished income capacity created a difficult situation for many local governments. Despite the reduction in revenue, local governments continued to shoulder the same level of local welfare and development expenditures (Wong and Bhattasali 2003). They were also responsible for keeping a balanced budget. In this conjuncture, tobacco tax bore special significance. Although several tobacco taxes were categorised as central tax, the tax on tobacco leaves – namely the special agricultural product tax – was classified as a local tax. The tax rate was 31%, the highest among all agricultural taxes. The high tax rate as well as its classification as a local tax therefore provided great incentives for local governments to promote tobacco cultivation.

The change in local finance coincided with a considerable price drop in the grain market in 1996, thus pushing peasants to grow more tobacco leaves to maintain their income. The concatenation of events (fiscal reform, local government promotion, drop in grain price) led to a surge in tobacco leaf production. By 1997 the overproduction of tobacco leaves became acute as the supply of tobacco leaves greatly exceeded cigarette demand. But since the practice of buying all tobacco leaves from peasants was still in place, local tobacco corporations and cigarette factories suffered from losses. As mentioned earlier, it was common for local tobacco corporations to purchase tobacco leaves far beyond the amounts specified in the contracts. This did not cause too much trouble in the 1980s because tobacco supply could match cigarette demand. However, although the number of smokers increased over the years following an increase in population, the continuously sharp rise in the supply of tobacco leaves eventually outweighed cigarette demand in the later 1990s. Tobacco leaves were piling up at an unprecedented rate in tobacco corporations and cigarette factories. For instance, in Guizhou the quota set by the STMA was a mere 7.8 million *dan*, but the actual production was more than 13 million *dan* (1 *dan* amounts to 50 kilograms). In such circumstances, some tobacco corporations had a large deficit and failed to pay for the purchases and had to issue IOUs (*da baitiao* 打白條).

The problem of overproduction and the financial implications were subsequently reflected in the national budget. According to the statistics, the central tobacco procurement plan was 45.4 million *dan* in 1997, but the actual amount purchased was 68.75 million *dan*. The national deficit incurred from tobacco leaf purchase was RMB 67 billion in 1998 (Zhang 2009).

However, a deficit in the national budget was not the main concern of local governments. In the wake of the soaring supply, local governments continued to press tobacco corporations and cigarette factories to purchase surplus tobacco leaves. Their main consideration, besides local revenue, was social stability. If tobacco corporations refused to buy tobacco leaves from peasants, the potential for peasant unrest was high. This can be reflected in the comments from an official of the Zunyi Cigarette Factory in Guizhou, one of the severely overproducing provinces: "The local government continued pushing us. What could you do when peasants were already producing so many leaves? If we did not collect them, there might have been a serious disturbance" (Interview, July 19, 2009). In essence, the purchase of surplus tobacco leaves from peasants amounted to a kind of subsidy for the tobacco growers. It was equivalent to an income transfer from the national revenue to the rural sector. The arrangement substantially improved the livelihood of peasants in the tobacco growing regions. Paradoxically, the original rationale for the establishment of a tobacco monopsony was to secure fiscal revenue for the national treasury. Yet under peculiar local governance and contradictory responsibilities, national monopsony turned out to be an important source of subsidy for local governments and peasants.

The Establishment of a New Regulatory Regime

The reverse flow of fiscal income eventually led the State Council to take action against unplanned tobacco procurement. A central notice was sent to authorities within the *tiao-kuai*, emphasising that the tobacco quota was a state mandatory plan and had to be strictly observed. Any purchase above the annual quota was forbidden.

A number of steps were taken by the State Council to strengthen its control over tobacco production. First of all, a dual control (*shuangkong* 雙控) policy was put in place. Under the policy, the tobacco planting areas and the amount of procurement were enforced according to contracts. Tobacco corporations were not allowed to purchase any surplus tobacco leaves beyond the contract, and peasants had to limit their planting area. Furthermore, the tax rate on tobacco leaves was reduced to 20%. Any extra subsidy provided by tobacco corporations was forbidden (Wang 2006).

In addition, the STMA carried out a so-called "planned planting based on market guidance" scheme in 1998. Under the scheme, cigarette factories were required to purchase tobacco leaves at the National Tobacco Leaf Trade Fair and to sign a letter of intent (LOI) with the tobacco corporations. The purchase amount was based on their assigned annual quota. Based on the LOI, the STMA formulated the tobacco planting plan, including the area and production amount, for each province. In making the plan, the STMA would take the past planting record into consideration and adjust the regional balance accordingly. After that, plantation figures would be broken down from the provincial level to the village level. Tobacco corporations at the lowest level would sign the procurement contract with tobacco peasants in accordance with the planting plan. The new tobacco leaf trading structure is presented in Figure 2.

An even more important reform was the alteration in organisational control after China's accession to the World Trade Organisation (WTO). Before the reform, tobacco corporations were under the significant influence of local governments because the latter had substantial control over the personnel appointment of corporation managers. Corporation managers were often obliged to collude with local cigarette factories to purchase locally produced cigarettes. Under the organisational reform in 2005, a new structure of parent-subsidiary hierarchy was institutionalised within the entire tobacco corporation system. Within this new structure, each corporation enjoyed limited autonomy in terms of its disposal of corporate assets. The power of personnel appointment was now vested in the hands of the parent corporation rather than in those of the local government. The influence of local governments on tobacco operation was therefore greatly reduced.

Under the new regime, the influence of the *tiao* has been substantially increased at the expense of the *kuai*. Local authorities cannot manipulate tobacco corporations as they did before. On the contrary, they have to meet the demands of tobacco corporations in order to

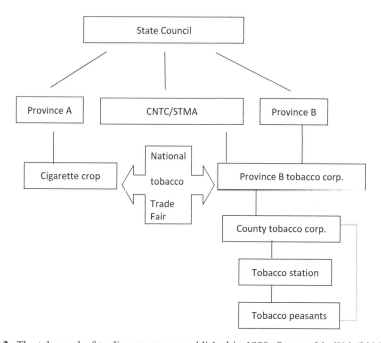

Figure 2. The tobacco leaf trading structure established in 1998. *Source*: Liu Wei (2005, 178).

share the tobacco revenues. These demands are laid down in duty contracts (*zeren zhuang* 責任狀) signed by the local government and its immediate (one level down) subordinates, and have become the criteria of performance evaluation for local authorities. In general, duty contracts are passed down the administrative hierarchy from municipal governments to village committees, with more and more detailed evaluation indices further down the command chain. This arrangement introduces a vigorous system of administrative accountability. It reverses the behaviour of local authorities from responding to local needs to obeying higher-level administrative instructions. An example of such requirements is given in Table 2. In this example the duty contract was signed between Town DJ and its subordinate village committees (VCs) in Yunnan Province in 2008.

From Table 2 we can see that village committees are encouraged not only to meet specific production quantities in certain tobacco cultivation areas but also to cultivate tobacco leaves according to specifications laid down. With China's accession to the WTO, a strategy of tobacco development has gradually taken shape under the CNTC's initiative. This involves

Table 2. Evaluation indices on tobacco farming

Evaluation index	Rewards and penalties
Accomplishing planting quotas and excluding inferior species	– Awarding RMB 1,500–2,000 to the village committees – Penalising the VCs RMB 1,000 for failure to achieve targeted planting quotas
Executing commercial tobacco seeding in floating trays	– Penalising the VCs RMB 1,000 for failure on this index and compensating RMB 5 for each seeding tray – If the VCs meet the index, neither penalty nor reward incentive is provided
Executing the best transplanting time from floating trays to farmland	– Awarding RMB 500 when the VCs ensure that tobacco seed transplantation is completed within three days during the prime planting season
Executing the expansion of scale planting by combining individual farmland in the same area	– Awarding RMB 200 for each parcel of tobacco farmland bigger than 100 *mu* (1 *mu* = 667 square metres) – Awarding RMB 100 for each lot of tobacco farmland bigger than 50 *mu*
Fulfilling the tobacco procurement amount	– Awarding RMB 1,500–2,000 to each VC for successful fulfilment of plan – Penalising the VC RMB 200 for every 1,000 kilograms below the procurement amount
Implementing safety regulations for tobacco flue-curing	– Awarding RMB 1,000–1,500 to each VC without any fire accidents caused by tobacco flue-curing – Penalising RMB 500 for each fire accident caused by tobacco flue-curing
Flue-cured tobacco leaves of superior/ medium quality	– Awarding RMB 4 to each VC and RMB 2 to each village group for every *dan* of superior/medium quality tobacco leaves once the VC fulfils the procurement amount and the proportion of superior/ medium quality is over 50%
Exclusive award for village party branch secretary (the first person in charge)	– The township government gives an exclusive award to the village party branch secretaries who achieve all the evaluation indices

improving the quality of tobacco, increasing the productivity of tobacco plantations, encouraging the formation of big cigarette enterprises and the establishment of national brand names in order to compete with foreign cigarette companies in the future. Subsequently, a project called "Establishing Modern Tobacco Agriculture" was formalised in 2007. This includes scale planting and commercial seeding, which are implemented through evaluation indices in duty contracts. Examples of such indices can be found in Table 2.

Local Governance under Conflicting Responsibilities

The implementation of the duty contracts has far-reaching implications for local governance. Local governments have been entrusted with conflicting responsibilities: they need to restore the efficacy of the tobacco monopsony, help modernise tobacco production, maintain budgetary balance and protect peasant welfare so as to maintain rural stability. These tasks need to be logical and consistent to improve governance, but in practice they are frequently at odds with one another because they demand different institutional responses from the local government.

A major example of the institutional response of the local government is revenue incentives. In 2005 the central government abolished the agricultural tax and the special agricultural product tax in order to reduce the tax burden on peasants. The tobacco leaf tax, as the only exception, was not abolished with other agricultural taxes. The tax rate has remained at 20%, and is classified as a local tax. This has specific implications for tobacco growing areas where local governments have to rely on the tobacco leaf tax, monetary rewards from evaluation indices and transfer payments.

In some cases, the transfer payment from higher-level governments has become a source of revenue for local governments (Göbel 2010). However, for many others the tobacco leaf tax and monetary rewards from evaluation indices remain by far the most important source of income. In Town HW of Yunnan Province, for example, the tobacco tax constituted 90% of local fiscal revenue in 2008 (Interview with party secretary in Town HW, December 2, 2008). In such circumstances it is not surprising to find growing conflicts between local governments and tobacco peasants when tax exaction becomes increasingly heavy-handed.

To begin with, the growing of tobacco has been a focal point of contention. The declining profitability of tobacco leaves makes some peasants reluctant to engage in the cultivation of tobacco. Under the new regulatory regime, the income and profits of tobacco peasants have generally declined since 1997, as shown in Table 3. Part of the reason for the substantial drop is as a result of the abolition of subsidies from tobacco corporations and cigarette enterprises. Many peasants are thus inclined to switch to other

Table 3. The profit-to-cost ratio of tobacco per *mu* (1996–2004)

	1996	1997	1998	1999	2000	2001	2002	2003	2004
Gross output value (RMB)	1,379.9	1,046.3	789.9	959.2	861.8	915.0	1,053.7	1,026.6	1,259.4
Gross cost (RMB)	839.9	858.15	815.9	772.4	793.0	811.3	873.6	859.1	1,072.0
Net profit (RMB)	539.8	188.1	−26.1	186.8	68.8	103.7	180.1	167.4	187.4
Profit-to-cost ratio (%)	64.3	21.9	−3.2	24.2	8.7	12.8	20.6	19.5	17.5

Source: STMA, cited in Wang, M. (2006, 30).

crops. However, local authorities have a strong interest in maintaining the planting of tobacco for the sake of retaining the tobacco tax revenue.

Some other tasks specified in the duty contracts have become another source of conflict, especially when such tasks have been carried out vigorously by local authorities at the expense of other considerations and governance responsibilities. For instance, in order to meet the assigned quotas under the plan, local cadres persuade and compel peasants to grow tobacco.[6] In principle, contract farming is based on an agreement signed by mutual consent. In practice, however, peasants have little choice but to grow tobacco if their farmlands have been included in the tobacco zone under the local plan. Otherwise they may be asked to vacate their farmland, as a local cadre in Town ZW explains:

If peasants don't want to grow tobacco, we will still continue to exercise influence over them in any way possible. For example, we can exchange farmland so that he or she will be able to grow other products on another piece of land. Or we can persuade the person concerned to rent the land to someone else who is willing to grow tobacco (Interview with party cadre in Town ZW, May 27, 2009).

It follows that the inclusion of a piece of farmland in the tobacco zone constitutes another source of contention. Since scale planting is a major goal of STMA in its strategic project, combining individual plots into large tracts of arable land for tobacco planting has become one of the key criteria for performance evaluation. In addition, local governments receive additional subsidies from tobacco corporations for an irrigation system and road construction if they meet the criteria of scale planting (Interview with party cadre in Yunnan, September 9, 2009). As a result, peasants are not only compelled to grow tobacco in the tobacco zone but also to combine their farmlands for scale cultivation.

There is another source of conflict that arises from the governance regime. Local governments and peasants clash over the practice of intercropping. Intercropping refers to the growing of two or more crops simultaneously on the same field. This is a common practice in many rural areas in China. Intercropping produces a greater yield on a given piece of land and hence increases the income of the cultivating household. Such a practice, however, is prohibited by local authorities in order to increase the proportion of superior quality tobacco leaves which is one of the evaluation criteria in the performance assessment. Such a prohibition not only limits peasants' planting freedom but also adversely affects their income. As a matter of fact, many peasants are still willing to grow tobacco despite the unfavourable selling price because the market risk is low under the monopoly system (Wang 2007). Yet almost every tobacco peasant would like to augment other crops with tobacco to raise his/her family income (Hu et al. 2008). The prohibition on intercropping thus arouses serious opposition from the peasants. To ease the discontent, some governments have allowed tobacco peasants to introduce intercropping in the late harvest season (Interview with tobacco peasant in Yunnan, August 23, 2009).

A further source of friction exists between peasants, tobacco corporations and local governments under the grading system. After flue-curing, tobacco leaves are brought to a local tobacco station where they are purchased according to a grading system issued by the STMA. However, this setup has been severely criticised for unfair grading. Peasants may obtain a better grade for their tobacco produce if they have a personal relationship with the grader or a poor grade if they do not. Some peasants respond to such an unfair system by selling their tobacco to smugglers or another station, which may invite intervention from local authorities. Local cadres are concerned that such illegal sales will affect the production quota. As a local official in Town DJ points out: "Meeting the tobacco purchase amount is the most important target we have to achieve. Otherwise we will be punished. We will try every means to meet the quota, even to the point of buying tobacco leaves from smugglers" (Interview, September 29, 009).

Paradoxically, the official combating of illegal sales of tobacco leaves is not always carried out strictly. The main reason is that the practice offers a certain degree of flexibility in the enforcement of the tobacco regime. Unlike industrial production, agricultural yield is always characterised by a high degree of uncertainty because of climatic fluctuations. When production output greatly exceeds the contract requirement, the purchase by smugglers becomes a very important channel for absorbing the surplus, and vice versa. The practice of illegal sales therefore plays a certain role in maintaining rural stability in the tobacco growing regions under the new regulatory regime.

Under fiscal considerations, carrying out the duty contracts to the fullest is now a "political mission" for local governments, one which must be completed by all administrative means available. In such circumstances, the locus of leverage has shifted. Instead of pulling the strings for tobacco corporations, local authorities have now become the observant agents of tobacco corporations. A cadre in Town DJ comments cynically on such a relationship: "It would seem that our main job is to serve the tobacco corporation. We must finish the job assigned by the tobacco corporation so that we can receive the money. It is a very important income for us" (Interview, September 9, 2009). Tobacco corporations are therefore able to shift the political pressure onto local governments. In principle they are responsible for enforcing the production contracts signed by the peasants. According to the procurement contract, if a peasant fails to implement the contract, the tobacco corporation will not renew the contract the next year. In practice, however, tobacco corporations are not seriously worried that peasants will be unable to complete the procurement contracts. This is because the responsibility for fulfilling the procurement contracts has already been transferred to the local authorities. Through a reward and punishment arrangement, tobacco corporations have institutionalised their leverage in manipulating local authorities to work for them. The duty contract has become an effective instrument in ensuring local compliance.

The new regulatory regime has fundamentally changed the relationship between local governments, tobacco corporations, cigarette factories and the peasants. The collusion between these local actors in manipulating the tobacco monopsony has been halted. Their common interests in retaining local tobacco incomes at the expense of the national treasury have been disrupted. Faced with the contradictory responsibilities of balancing their budget versus protecting the livelihood of peasants, local governments have turned their back on the peasants. The grievances of the peasants are contained through an informal toleration of smuggling and illegal tobacco sales.

Conclusion

It has been widely acknowledged that bureaucratic performance is closely linked to good institutional setups. In the context of developing countries, the quality of bureaucratic rule shapes bureaucratic performance, which in turn influences development outcomes (Hyden, Court, and Mease 2004). In addition to meritocracy, administrative accountability and transparency are among the most important factors believed to be closely related to the quality of bureaucratic rule, and hence good governance. Our case study on China shows that this is not so straightforward.

Bureaucratic rule in China at the grass-roots level is shaped by an incentive system as well as by the discretionary power of local officials. In general, the Chinese central government ensures that local authorities will pursue the "national interests" defined by Beijing through its control of local appointments and through its manipulation of fiscal incentives. However, the lapse in such a control system due to the fragmentation of authority generates conflicting responsibilities for local governments within the administrative matrix. The result is a surge of local government capacity, which has caught the attention of observers (Chien 2013). Some see it as an exemplar of decentralised governance; others view it as a kind of "decentralised predation."

Nonetheless, such slippage may not always result in undesirable outcomes. Our case study of the tobacco growing areas reveals a more ambivalent situation. The tobacco regime has undergone two distinctive phases of operation. During the first phase, many of the fiscal and administrative decisions were deconcentrated and devolved. But the power and influence between the deconcentrated administrative hierarchy and the devolved territorial authorities was uneven. As a result, local authorities made good use of their discretionary power in sabotaging the monopsony. From the perspective of the state, the enforcement of administrative accountability in the tobacco system was weak and bureaucratic discipline was poor. Yet local governments were responsive to local needs and were able to manoeuvre the system in such a way as to bring direct subsidy to the peasants and to fuel local development. This stands in stark contrast to the second phase, when a more "effective" state monopsony was established. A stricter set of rules was promulgated, and clear lines of command were put in place. Power and influence was tilted in favour of the line hierarchy at the expense of territorial authorities. Under this new arrangement, bureaucratic performance could be evaluated with effective criteria, while responsible cadres could be held accountable for their performance. Ironically, the enforcement of such an arrangement, with supposedly more transparency and better quality of bureaucratic rule, has placed state interests in direct conflict with peasants' interests and local welfare.

This case study reminds us that a more nuanced understanding of good governance and bureaucratic responsibility is needed in analysing countries where the lines of authority are diffuse and the rules of the game are not constructed along principles of democratic competition. It is a truism to say that good governance is desirable, but the case study clearly shows there is no linear relationship between elements of good governance and governance outcomes, given the specific institutional embeddedness of China's tobacco growing areas. It reminds us that continuous dialogues between universal principles and concrete historical realities are needed in order to gauge the relevance of the concept.

Acknowledgments

An earlier version of this article was presented at the International Workshop on "Good Governance in the Asia-Pacific Region: Civil and Political Society," City University of Hong Kong, 9–10 December 2010. We are grateful for the comments from the participants. We are particularly thankful to Linda Li and the anonymous reviewers of JCA for their invaluable suggestions.

Notes

[1] In the following discussions, we will focus mainly on the procurement of tobacco leaves and thus make reference to the monopsony aspect of the tobacco regime.

[2] Before 2003, the State Planning Commission was the central planning authority. It was reorganised into the National Development and Reform Commission in 2003.

[3] Again, the set of regulations on tobacco procurement has remained the same since the *Tobacco Monopoly Law* took effect in 1992.

[4] Before 1984, local governments collected a 40% industrial-commercial tax on tobacco leaves. As of 1984 this became a production tax.

[5] For example, Honghe Prefecture of Yunnan Province asked all the counties to remit 30% of beyond-production tobacco leaves so that it could share the profits.

[6] In order to sustain peasants' motivation for growing tobacco, some local governments also appropriate the funding from tobacco leaf taxation to subsidise peasants in the tobacco cultivation process.

References

Alpermann, B. 2010. *China's Cotton Industry: Economic Transformation and State Capacity.* London: Routledge.

Brenner, N. 1998. "Global Cities, Glocal States: Global City Formation and State Territorial Restructuring in Contemporary Europe." *Review of International Political Economy* 5 (1): 1–37.

Cheema, G., and D. Rondinelli. 2007. "From Government Decentralization to Decentralized Governance." In *Decentralizing Governance Emerging Concepts and Practices*, edited by G. Cheema and D. Rondinelli, 1–20. Washington, DC: Brookings Institution Press.

Chibber, V. 2003. *Locked in Place: State-Building and Late Industrialization in India.* Princeton: Princeton University Press.

Chien, S. 2013. "Chinese Eco-Cities: A Perspective of Land-Speculation-Oriented Local Entreprenerialism." *China Information* 27 (2): 173–196.

Davoodi, H., and H. Zou. 1998. "Fiscal Decentralization and Economic Growth: A Cross-Country Study." *Journal of Urban Economics* 43: 244–257.

Dirlik, A. 2012. "The Idea of a 'Chinese Model': A Critical Discussion." *China Information* 26 (3): 277–302.

Edin, M. 2000. *Market Forces and Communist Power: Local Political Institutions and Economic Development in China.* Uppsala: Uppsala University Press.

Evans, P. 1995. *Embedded Autonomy: States and Industrial Transformation.* Princeton: Princeton University Press.

Gao, J. 2009. "Governing by Goals and Numbers: A Case Study in the Use of Performance Measurement to Build State Capacity in China." *Public Administration and Development* 29 (1): 21–31.

Göbel, C. 2010. *The Politics of Rural Reform in China: State Policy and Village Predicament in the Early 2000s.* London: Routledge.

Grindle, M. 2004. "Good Enough Governance: Poverty Reduction and Reform in Developing Countries." *Governance* 17 (4): 525–548.

Grindle, M. 2009. *Going Local: Decentralization, Democratization, and the Promise of Good Governance.* Princeton: Princeton University Press.

Hu, T., Z. Mao, J. Shi, and W. Chen. 2008. *Zhongguo De Yancao Shuishou Ji Qi Qianzai De Jingji Yingxiang" [China's Tobacco Taxation and Its Potential Economic Influence].* Paris: International Union Against Tuberculosis and Lung Diseases.

Hyden, G., J. Court, and K. Mease. 2004. *Making Sense of Governance: Empirical Evidence From 16 Developing Countries.* London: Lynne Rienner.

Irwin Crookes, P. 2012. "China's New Development Model: Analysing Chinese Prospects in Technology Innovation." *China Information* 26 (2): 167–184.

Johnson, C. 1982. *MITI and the Japanese Miracle: The Growth of Industrial Policy, 1925–1975.* Stanford: Stanford University Press.

Lange, A. 2010. "Elites in Local Development in the Philippines." *Development and Change* 41 (1): 53–76.

Liu, W. 2005. *Jingi Zhuangui Guocheng Zhong De Chanye Chongzu: Yi Yancaoye Wei Li [The Industrial Reorganization Under Economic Transition: Taking Tobacco Industry as an Example).* Beijing: China Social Science Press.

Martinez-Vazquez, J., and R. McNab. 2003. "Fiscal Decentralization and Economic Growth." *World Development* 31 (9): 1597–1616.

Mattlin, M. 2011. *Politicized Society: The Long Shadow of Taiwan's One-Party Legacy.* Copenhagen: NIAS Press.

Mertha, A. 2005. "China's 'Soft' Centralization: Shifting *Tiao/Kuai* Authority Relations." *The China Quarterly* 184: 791–810.

Montinola, G., Y. Qian, and B. Weingast. 1995. "Federalism, Chinese Style: The Political Basis for Economic Success in China." *World Politics* 48 (1): 50–81.

Ngo, T.-W. 2004. "'Bad Governance' Under Democratic Rule in Taiwan." In *Good Governance in the Era of Global Neoliberalism*, edited by J. Demmers, A. Fernández Jilberto and B. Hogenboom, 224–245. London: Routledge.

Ngo, T.-W. 2006. "Possible and Impossible Games: Institutional Order and Social Conflicts in Argentina and Taiwan." In *Political Conflict and Development in East Asia and Latin America*, edited by R. Boyd, B. Galjart and T.-W. Ngo, 118–147. London: Routledge.

Oi, J. 1999. *Rural China Takes Off: Institutional Foundations of Economic Reform*. Berkeley: University of California Press.

Pei, M. 2006. *China's Trapped Transition: The Limits of Developmental Autocracy*. Cambridge: Harvard University Press.

Peng, Y. 1996. "The Politics of Tobacco: Relations Between Farmers and Local Governments in China's Southwest." *The China Journal* 36: 67–82.

Waldner, D. 1999. *State Building and Late Development*. Ithaca: Cornell University Press.

Wang, M. 2006. "Yanye Shougou Zhengce Yu Yannong Liyi Fenxi Ji Jianyi" [The Tobacco Procurement Policy and Tobacco Peasants' Interests: Analysis and Suggestions]." *Nongcun Caizheng Yu Caiwu [Rural Fiscal Polity and Finance]* 12: 30–31.

Wang, X. 2007. "Yanye Zhuanmaipin De Shichanghua Gaige Ji Zhengce Tiaozheng Quxiang" [Tobacco Leaf Marketization Reform and Policy Shift]. PhD Diss., Chinese Academy of Agricultural Sciences.

Wang, H. 2009. "Zhuanmai Zhidu Xia Woguo Yancao Chanye De Gaige Yu Fazhan" [Tobacco Industry Reform and Development Under the Monopoly System)." *Shanghai Jingji Yanjiu [Shanghai Economic Review]* 4: 22–28.

Whiting, S. 2000. *Power and Wealth in Rural China: The Political Economy of Institutional Change*. 1st ed. Cambridge: Cambridge University Press.

Wong, C. 1991. "Central-Local Relations in an Era of Fiscal Decline: The Paradox of Fiscal Decentralization in Post-Mao China." *The China Quarterly* 128: 691–715.

Wong, C., and D. Bhattasali. 2003. *Zhuogguo: Guojia Fazhan Yu Difang Caizheng [China: National Development and Sub-National Finance]*. Translated into Chinese by S. Wu and G. Wang. Beijing: China Citic Press.

Yang, D. 2004. *Remaking the Chinese Leviathan: Market Transition and the Politics of Governance in China*. Stanford, CA: Stanford University Press.

Yang, A. 2009. *Zhongguo Yancao Tongzhi [The Annals of Chinese Tobacco]*. Beijing: Zhonghua Book Company.

Yang, Z., and Z. Yang. 2008. *Zhongguo Caizheng Zhidu Gaige Sanshi Nian [The Thirty Years of Fiscal Reform in China]*. Shanghai: Truth and Wisdom Press.

Zhang, J. 2009. "*Nian Yanye Da Chaochan De Tiaozheng*" [The Adjustment of the Tobacco Leaf Overproduction in 1997], *Zhongguo Yancao Zixun Wang* [China Tobacco Information Website]. Accessed December 15. http://www.echinatobacco.com/101588/102041/102524/43610.html

Good Governance for Environmental Protection in China: Instrumentation, Strategic Interactions and Unintended Consequences

THOMAS JOHNSON

Department of Public Policy, City University of Hong Kong, Kowloon, Hong Kong SAR

ABSTRACT *During the past decade, China's Ministry of Environmental Protection has pursued a strategy of "extending governance" to the public by creating formal public participation channels and promoting environmental transparency. Rather than representing a normative end in their own right, these features of "good governance" are being used instrumentally by the political executive to enlist public support in enforcing environmental regulations, and to depoliticise dissent by channelling it through legal mechanisms. This paper examines how environmental non-governmental organisations and "not-in-my-backyard" movements strategically interact with the Ministry of Environmental Protection and its good governance rhetoric to promote their own objectives. At the same time, it argues that unintended consequences have emerged as Chinese citizens increasingly assert their participatory and transparency "rights." By appropriating instrumental good governance policies to their own advantage, citizens define concepts such as participation and transparency on their own terms.*

Faced with a serious and unprecedented environmental challenge, the Chinese central government has progressively strengthened environmental protection laws and institutions, and diversified environmental policy instruments (Mol and Carter 2006). One key aspect of these environmental governance reforms has been the attempt to enlist public support in tackling polluters and unruly local officials under whose watch egregious environmental degradation frequently occurs. Starting in 2003, the central government has introduced laws and regulations that provide legal channels for public participation and information disclosure as part of a "public supervision mechanism" (*shehui jiandu jizhi*) (State Council 2005). Formal channels for soliciting public comment in planning decisions have been established under the Environmental Impact Assessment (EIA) and Administrative Licensing (AL) Laws (both effective since 2003). Moreover, local governments and enterprises in violation of pollution laws and regulations are required to disclose certain types of environmental information, following the 2008 Measures on Environmental Information Disclosure (Trial Version) (MEID). At first glance, the aim of the public supervision mechanism appears to be the introduction of greater accountability, transparency, predictability and participation in environmental governance. Elsewhere, these qualities have been defined as institutional features of "good governance" (World Bank 1992).

The "good governance" concept became prominent in the late 1980s when certain aid donors insisted that recipient countries adopt good governance practices, ostensibly to maximise the effectiveness of developmental aid. Although a set of objective criteria for measuring the concept is lacking, various subjective criteria have been identified (Nanda 2006). Accountability is premised on the ability of government officials to answer for their actions and be responsive to the public (Asian Development Bank 1995; Sibbel 2005). Transparency means that the rules and functions by which a government operates are clear, and that information should be accessible to the public through channels including a free media and legislation that compels public officials to release information (Asian Development Bank 1995; Sibbel 2005). Predictability is closely associated with the rule of law. It means that laws, regulations and policies are in place to regulate society, and are applied fairly and consistently to state and non-state actors (Asian Development Bank 1995). Finally, participation involves providing a role for the public in development, including individuals and intermediary organisations such as non-governmental organisations (NGOs). It is based on the assumption that governance can be improved if those affected by development can also influence events as agents of development (Asian Development Bank 1995).

Critics have claimed that the World Bank and other donors have used good governance criteria instrumentally in order to legitimise the imposition of a neoliberal agenda on developing countries (Cammack 2004). Rather than giving the public agency in development issues, good governance promotes a form of "controlled participation" that is largely inconsequential to outcomes (Cammack 2004; Mercer 2003; Cornwall and Brock 2005). Concepts such as participation, empowerment and transparency are in reality often little more than "buzzwords" that have been co-opted by international organisations to serve their own goals and depoliticise societal contestation (Cornwall and Brock 2005; Jayasuriya and Hewison 2004).

With this in mind, how should we interpret the introduction of "good governance" practices in environmental policy in an unambiguously illiberal regime that simultaneously restricts civic and political rights in order to maintain one-party rule? This paper argues that the public supervision mechanism has been facilitated by wider ongoing administrative reforms within the central government that emphasise good governance principles such as rule of law, transparency and public participation. Rather than representing the part of the normative "good governance" agenda designed to foster political liberalisation, institutional features of "good governance" are being introduced instrumentally to legitimise Chinese Communist Party (CCP) rule and depoliticise civil society (Pieke 2012). Certain "reformist" officials within China's Ministry of Environmental Protection (MEP) have utilised this broader commitment to "good governance" principles to advance a public participation agenda within the existing political process that they hope can improve environmental policy implementation and bolster the MEP's standing relative to powerful economic ministries. MEP officials have entered into mutually beneficial "strategic interactions" with several environmental NGOs (ENGOs) to improve institutional conditions for public participation (a key goal for many green groups) whilst achieving their own organisational aims. These strategic interactions have raised the public supervision mechanism's public profile, and have sometimes helped ENGOs exert limited external oversight over polluters. Yet in reality, China's public supervision mechanism is a weak tool that can at best facilitate tokenistic participation with a negligible impact on environmental outcomes. At the same time, some not-in-my-back-yard (NIMBY) campaigners have appropriated the public supervision mechanism to their own ends by interpreting legal participatory and transparency provisions in the language of "rights." Rather than being satisfied with the mere opportunity to participate via institutional channels, as some ENGOs appear to be, NIMBY actors tend to adopt a more expansive definition of good governance. Because they mobilise reactively in defence of their own health and/or financial interests, NIMBY actors are especially persistent in pressing officials to respect their "right" to be consulted over locally-unwanted-land-uses (LULUs). These new bottom-up pressures for a more substantial vision of good governance with meaningful as opposed to tokenistic participation are unintended consequences of the central government's administrative reforms.

"Good Governance" and China's Administrative Reforms

Chinese interest in the concept of "good governance" was stoked by the publication and subsequent translation into Chinese of the 1992 World Bank Annual Report entitled "Governance and Development." According to Zheng Yongnian (2006), the CCP leadership became interested in pursuing good governance during the reform and opening-up era as its source of legitimacy shifted from communist dogma towards governing competency. Zhang Weiwei (2006) claims that a consensus emerged among the country's leadership that promoting a managerial form of good governance by cultivating rule of law, increasing media supervision and improving supervision over government institutions is necessary, and is also seen as preferable to introducing a model of Western liberal democracy (see also Heberer and Schubert 2006).

The spirit of good governance has been embodied in many recent government policies, and some Chinese commentators have closely linked it to the much more prominent "Harmonious Society" rhetoric promoted by the Hu/Wen leadership (Zhang 2007; also see Yu 2006). The central government has taken steps to encourage managerial competency, organisational capacity, accountability, rule of law, transparency and public participation, within the context of a one-party state (Xue and Liou 2012). This has been embodied in, for example, the 2004 State Council "Comprehensive Strategy to Implement the Promotion of Administration According to Law," as well as the 2007 "People's Republic of China Ordinance on Governmental Information Disclosure" (hereinafter referred to as the "PRC Information Disclosure Ordinance") and e government initiatives that promote government transparency (State Council 2007). Citizen participation has been facilitated via village elections and, more recently, public hearings that have mainly focused on the setting of urban water tariffs and train ticket prices (Zhong and Mol 2008; Xue and Liou 2012). Jun Ma (2012) has labelled these top-down reforms as examples of "state-led" social accountability. He distinguishes them from "society-led" social accountability, which involves ordinary citizens holding officials accountable through, for example, social movements, NGOs and internet campaigns (Ma 2012).

Frank Pieke (2012) has viewed these administrative reforms as an attempt to facilitate greater pluralism whilst simultaneously strengthening the CCP's leading role over society. One key aim is to channel growing popular unrest within the system, depoliticise civil society and maintain social stability in response to the growing societal diversification of the reform era (Pieke 2012). According to this view, the aim of these administrative reforms is to maintain the CCP's grip on power amid significant social and economic change.

"Good Governance" as Instrumentalism: China's Public Supervision Mechanism

China began to establish its "environmental state," which includes environmental laws, policies and governing institutions, in the early 1970s (Mol and Carter 2006). Whilst Chinese environmental legislation had become relatively comprehensive by the 2000s, the highly decentralised nature of enforcement has led predominantly to weak implementation by environmental protection bureaus (EPBs) which answer first and foremost to local governments that tend to prioritise economic growth (Jahiel 1997; Economy 2005; Van Rooij 2006; Mol and Carter 2006).

More recently however, the central government has accorded greater priority to environmental issues. Growing concern for environmental and resource issues has been expressed in numerous high-level speeches and documents, and is reflected in ambitious pollution reduction and energy efficiency targets found in the 11th and 12th Five-Year Plans covering the 2006–15 period. In the past decade, China's State Environmental Protection Administration (SEPA), long seen as a weak department, became more assertive in holding local officials accountable for implementing environmental legislation.[1] Enforcement of EIA procedures became a key focus for SEPA officials, who decried the tendency of local governments and powerful economic ministries to forego proper EIA procedures in relation to new projects. Between 2005 and 2007 SEPA launched three "environmental storms," in which it implemented high-profile crackdowns on large-scale construction projects that had violated the EIA Law. Yet although the environmental storm initiatives temporarily halted several major projects and raised SEPA's profile, this campaign-style approach to environmental enforcement only represented a short-term fix, and many projects continue to proceed without taking EIA seriously.

Some SEPA officials have therefore argued that China can only overcome weak policy implementation through enabling the public to "supervise" local officials. China's broader administrative reforms provided "legal authorisation" that enabled SEPA to advance a public participation agenda designed to boost transparency and enlist public support in improving policy implementation (Interview with Peking University academic, June 26, 2012). Rather than representing a new direction for SEPA as a whole, this agenda was promoted by certain "reformist and enlightened" officials within the agency, who viewed constraints on public participation and transparency as obstacles to environmental protection (Interview with MEP official, June 21, 2012). However, as Andrew Mertha (2008) found in his study of Chinese hydropower politics, these "policy entrepreneurs" prefer to work within the existing political process rather than against it. Chief among them was SEPA Vice-Minister Pan Yue, who also spearheaded the three environmental storms. Pan stated that "the ultimate force for resolving China's serious environmental problems comes from the public" (*China News Online*, April 1, 2007). Yet he also acknowledged that a dearth of institutionalised participatory channels had undermined environmental public participation in China. In Pan's words, "insufficient legal mechanisms for public participation are an important reason why China's environmental protection has laws that are not enforced, as well as having laws that are enforced in a lax manner" (Pan 2004). To remedy this situation, SEPA began establishing a legal framework for public participation, which has been referred to as a "public supervision mechanism" (see Table 1) (State Council 2005). It was hoped that this would facilitate greater public supervision of unruly local officials through enhancing state-led social accountability.

So far, the public supervision mechanism incorporates three main strands: incorporating public opinion into planning decisions, improving environmental transparency and promoting environmental public interest litigation (State Council 2005). Due to space constraints, this paper focuses on the first two strands. The EIA Law states that public opinion "should" (*yingdang*) be solicited for projects liable to have significant public impact. This also applies to the granting of licences under the AL Law. Both these laws state that the

Table 1. Key public participation and transparency legislation

Legislation/regulation	Date effective	Promulgating agency	Relevance
Environmental Impact Assessment Law	2003	National People's Congress (NPC)	Public should be consulted over projects that affect them
Administrative Licensing Law	2003	NPC	Public can apply for a public hearing over licensing decisions that affect them
Notice Regarding the Carrying Out of Environmental Protection Checks by Companies Applying to be Listed, and by Listed Companies Applying for Refinancing	2003	SEPA	Companies applying for listing must provide environmental information to local environmental authorities
Temporary Measures for Public Participation in Administrative Licensing Hearings	2004	SEPA	Clarifies how and when public should be consulted over an administrative licensing decision
State Council Decision Regarding Implementing the Scientific Development Concept and Strengthening Environmental Protection	2005	State Council	Calls for improved social supervision, transparency, advocates public interest litigation and public hearings; public participation should be facilitated
Temporary Measures for Public Participation in Environmental Impact Assessment	2006	SEPA	Clarifies how and when public should be consulted over an EIA
Temporary Measures on Environmental Information Disclosure	2008	SEPA	Outlines 17 types of environmental information that should be publicly disclosed
Water Pollution Control and Prevention Law	2008	NPC	Citizens can sue for damages caused by water pollution; NGOs and lawyers can support litigants

public may be consulted via mechanisms such as public hearings, questionnaires and/or opinion surveys. Their implementing measures, promulgated by SEPA in 2004 and 2006 respectively, further clarify how public participation should proceed. Yet there are shortcomings in this legislation. For example, the term "public" is left undefined, allowing considerable scope for authorities to meet these public consultation requirements through soliciting opinions of, for example, experts or handpicked members of the public unlikely to oppose a certain project. In addition, the wording of the EIA Law suggests that public consultation is still voluntary and not mandatory. As a result, units responsible for conducting EIAs frequently "go through the motions" (*zou guochang*) and treat public participation as a box-ticking exercise, rather than an opportunity to facilitate meaningful participation (Qie 2011).

During the past decade the central government has also attempted to improve environmental transparency. Since 2003 it has increased environmental disclosure requirements for companies applying for initial public offerings (IPOs), and has provided opportunities for the public to comment on IPO applications. According to the 2003 "Notice Regarding the Carrying Out of Environmental Protection Checks by Companies Applying to be Listed, and by Listed Companies Applying for Refinancing" (referred to as the "2003 Notice"), companies applying for stock market listing must first obtain approval from the environmental agency based on their environmental records, before their listing applications can be approved by the China Securities Regulatory Commission (SEPA 2003). Companies must provide environmental information to the authorities covering the 36-month period prior to their IPO application. If they violate environmental legislation during this time they should be prevented from conducting an IPO. Furthermore, in May 2008 the MEID, which was pursuant to the PRC Information Disclosure Ordinance, took effect. These measures require the disclosure of information by EPBs and enterprises that have violated environmental regulations. They also enable the public to apply to local governments for environmental information disclosure. Improving transparency is vital in empowering the public to help achieve SEPA's goal of holding officials and polluters accountable. As one SEPA official remarked, "environmental information disclosure … is beneficial for public supervision, and provides beneficial conditions for strengthening the enforcement of environmental legislation and overcoming local protectionism" (*China Environment News*, April 26, 2007). Despite this, the MEID also suffers from weak wording. For example, it defines information disclosure as something that companies and local officials "should" (*yingdang*), and not "must," do. In addition, there is considerable scope for information to be withheld ostensibly to protect state and/or company secrets.

The party-state's policy on public participation and transparency is not designed to give the public unlimited involvement in environmental issues, for example, by challenging the party-state's control over formulating environmental policies. Rather, the aim is to create "orderly participation" through a top-down mechanism that citizens can access to rein in unruly local officials and therefore serve the aims of the central government's environmental protection agency (Ma 2006; State Council 2005). In other words, the purpose of introducing "good governance" features in the environmental protection sphere is to enable the public to help SEPA achieve its operational mandate of protecting the environment, a mandate undermined by weak policy enforcement by local governments. Yet the promulgation of legislation to facilitate public participation is insufficient. The same officials charged with implementing this legislation are loath to encourage public supervision amounting to a check on their own power. As a result, public action is needed to bring SEPA's public participation agenda to life.

Strategic State–Society Interactions and Unintended Consequences

The question is whether, or to what extent, such narrowly instrumental objectives of the central state can be achieved, without letting loose other social processes and setting the scene for wider changes at the same time? This section examines, through several case studies, how ENGOs and NIMBY actors have responded to the MEP's public supervision mechanism to bring about a mix of consequences. The section discusses two cases of ENGO interaction with the public supervision mechanism. The first case discusses how ENGOs worked with SEPA in 2005, as the latter held China's first national-level environmental public hearing in relation to renovation work conducted at Yuanmingyuan (the Old Summer Palace). This case was selected because it was widely seen as an important early experiment in conducting public consultation for a controversial project. The second case shows how ENGOs pressurised the Gold East Paper Company over its environmental record during its application to conduct an IPO. This case was chosen because unlike the Yuanmingyuan case, ENGO activism was aimed at a corporation. In addition, this case occurred in 2008, by which time relations between SEPA and ENGO activists had dampened. Although these cases cannot be fully representative, they do show how ENGOs (sometimes in collaboration with SEPA) try to enforce the public supervision mechanism. Information for these two cases is derived from documentary sources, including newspaper reports, government documents and ENGO newsletters. In addition, I conducted 15 interviews between 2007 and 2012 with ENGO participants, government officials and Chinese academics.

ENGOs

A 2008 report by the All-China Environment Federation (ACEF) stated that China had over 500 "grass-roots" ENGOs (ACEF 2008). The vast majority of these practice self-censorship and maintain a low profile in order not to antagonise the party-state (Ho and Edmonds 2007). In some cases, ENGO activists enjoy close personal ties with party-state officials, leading some scholars to claim that Chinese environmental activism is "embedded" within the state (Ho and Edmonds 2007). Although the need to self-censor limits ENGOs' freedom to act, embeddedness enables green activists to exert influence by working with sympathetic officials. Not all ENGOs are "embedded" in the state, or are embedded to the same degree. Nevertheless, developing a similar "outlook" and a collaborative rather than conflicting relationship can provide green groups with access and influence to areas of public policy and decisions where and when interests between activists and officials coalesce.

The promotion of a good governance agenda through the top-down public supervision mechanism is an area of mutual interest for the MEP and ENGOs. Whilst the MEP needs the public supervision mechanism to bolster local execution of its environmental policy, ENGOs see an opportunity to extend the boundaries of the authoritarian political system and improve the institutional conditions for environmental activism (Johnson 2010). To achieve this goal of "turning laws on paper into laws implemented in reality" (Interview with Peking University academic, June 26, 2012), ENGOs have entered into "strategic interactions" with the MEP in promoting its good governance agenda.

The Yuanmingyuan Public Hearing

In 2003 local government agencies drafted plans to renovate Yuanmingyuan, a site of historical importance in Beijing. These plans included lining the site's numerous lakebeds and riverbeds with plastic to reduce water seepage. This project only became public knowledge in March 2005 after a concerned visitor alerted the media and Friends of Nature, a Beijing-based ENGO. On 31 March, SEPA stepped in and ordered renovation work to halt because no EIA had been conducted. A "make-up" (*buban*) EIA was ordered, and SEPA announced that China's first national-level environmental public hearing would be held to debate the issue.[2]

The Yuanmingyuan public hearing must be understood in the context of preceding environmental opposition to hydropower development on the Nu River in Yunnan Province. Since 2003, SEPA and ENGO activists had worked together to oppose the damming of the river, and had brought the issue to public attention (see Mertha 2008). SEPA officials initially planned to hold a public hearing to debate this highly contentious issue once the EIA Law became active in 2003. However, the pro-hydropower National Development and Reform Commission (NDRC) vetoed this move (Interview with ENGO founder, Beijing, June 20, 2012). When the Yuanmingyuan controversy emerged, SEPA then transferred its preparation work for the aborted Nu River public hearing to this far less contentious case (Interview with ENGO founder, Beijing, June 20, 2012).

From the pro-environmental actors' perspectives, the issue of renovations to Yuanmingyuan was relatively minor compared with hydropower development in an area of impressive biodiversity and natural beauty. Nevertheless, SEPA identified the significant public interest in the Yuanmingyuan case as a good opportunity to showcase its nascent public participation agenda. According to one official, "at that time ENGO and public attention [on the Yuanmingyuan issue] was substantial. *We decided to utilise this* to convene a public hearing, and meaningfully implement the Temporary Measures on Public Participation in EIA" (Interview with MEP official, June 21, 2012, emphasis added).[3] SEPA support for public involvement in the Nu River and Yuanmingyuan cases was a reflection of the will of individual leaders such as Pan Yue, who were committed to public participation. One MEP official claimed that "if different people were in post [at SEPA], the Nu River would have been developed ten times over, Yuanmingyuan would have been covered by ten layers of plastic" (Interview with MEP official, June 21, 2012).[4]

Several Beijing-based ENGOs helped SEPA showcase its legal framework for public participation. One ENGO activist involved in the case described this as a "very natural cooperation," given that expanding public participation was a common goal for ENGO activists and certain SEPA officials (Interview with ENGO activist, July 14, 2007). Liang Congjie, founder of the ENGO Friends of Nature, expressed strong support for a public hearing in conversations with SEPA officials (Interview with MEP official, June 21, 2012). Strategic interactions between ENGO activists and SEPA officials were facilitated by overlapping goals and personal connections (Interview with ENGO founder, June 20, 2012).

Before the public hearing, several green groups organised events that helped keep the Yuanmingyuan issue in the public eye. For example, Friends of Nature organised a "people's hearing" to generate debate several days before the official hearing (Interview with ENGO activist, July 14, 2007). Over 50 people attended, including academics, ENGO activists, journalists, members of the public and, in a show of support, one SEPA official. Several ENGOs also issued a statement criticising project overseers for ignoring EIA procedures and calling for a public hearing to be held (Friends of Nature 2005).

During the public hearing of 13 April, Pan Yue stated that its purpose was to expand and standardise public participation, and promote a more "democratic" decision-making process. It was seen as a test case in implementing the public supervision mechanism. As Pan stated,

> *In reality, we just want to do an exploration.* The government establishes an open platform and allows all kinds of opinions to collect and be exchanged. Through a kind of transparent and open forum, [we can] open up to society all of the relevant links in the government's decision-making, publicise decision-making content towards society in a timely manner, and make the government's administrative behaviour subject to public opinion and supervision. This is consistent with an administrative method of democratic decision-making, scientific decision-making, and is beneficial towards the building of a harmonious society (*Xinhua News Agency*, July 18, 2005, emphasis added).

Another official recounted that "without wanting to overestimate our abilities, we wanted to open a reform to the political system, [we wanted to open] an entry point for public participation" (Interview with MEP official, June 21, 2012). Over 120 people attended the hearing, and several ENGO participants contributed their views. In a show of transparency the hearing was broadcast live on the websites of *Xinhua* and the *People's Daily*, and the EIA report was subsequently uploaded to SEPA's website. Within 10 hours of appearing online, the report had received 17,000 hits, causing the website to crash (*Southern Weekend*, July 22, 2005).

From SEPA's perspective, ENGO participation added legitimacy to the process. Moore and Warren (2006, 9) argued that "in part due to national NGO participation, the Yuanmingyuan hearing involved greater attention to the public's procedural participation rights and implementation through hearing rules, as well as greater national publicity and increased attention to the [EIA] report's conclusions." ENGO participants viewed the public hearing as an important step towards their goal of expanding environmental public participation (Friends of Nature 2006). The value of the legal provision for public hearings for ENGO activists is that it enables them to legitimately "speak out" (*shuo shi'er*) and call for procedural justice in relation to the EIA process (Interview with ENGO founder, June 20, 2012). This was evident in the Nu River campaign, when ENGOs on two occasions called for a public hearing to be held, although to no avail (Johnson 2010).

Ironically, despite the enthusiasm stimulated by this exercise in public participation, the impact of ENGOs and of the hearing itself on the outcome of this case was negligible. The 90% of the project already completed was allowed to stand, stoking speculation that SEPA had made a political decision rather than embracing the outcome of "public supervision" (Moore and Warren 2006, 17). In addition, the hearing was only conducted after the EIA had been completed, not – as it should have been – before (Moore and Warren 2006). In short, the public hearing only brought forth a thin veneer of good governance – through raising public awareness about legal channels for public participation.

The Campaign Against the Gold East Paper Company

The Yuanmingyuan case featured close personal cooperation between SEPA officials and ENGO activists. The will of individual leaders (most notably Pan Yue) was important in promoting a public participation agenda that suited both parties. Yet by late 2007 Pan Yue, who once stated that ENGOs and SEPA officials "are all in the same family" (Young 2005), had reportedly been side-lined within SEPA (Interview with Peking University academic, June 26, 2012; *The Guardian*, March 12, 2009). This, along with the removal in 2005 of SEPA Minister Xie Zhenhua, dampened ENGO relations with the ministry (Interview with MEP official, June 21, 2012; Interview with ENGO activist, July 3, 2012). Although ENGOs continued to cooperate with SEPA, this was mainly with lower ranking officials (Interview with ENGO activist, July 3, 2012). Despite this, legislation for public participation and transparency has endured, as has the goal shared by many ENGOs of using it to promote reform within the system.

An ENGO campaign against the Gold East Paper Company (GEP) shows how activists have utilised the MEP's good governance agenda to improve oversight of enterprises. Compared with the Yuanmingyuan case, this campaign involved a more "tacit" (*moqi*) form of cooperation between lower-ranking MEP officials and ENGO activists (Interview with ENGO activist, July 3, 2012). Hence, despite reduced support from MEP leaders, relationships between ENGO activists and lower-level officials were such that cooperation could endure, albeit in a less high-profile manner. In the GEP case, although the former relayed information to the MEP through personal connections, they also attempted to hold GEP to the requirements of the public supervision mechanism (Interview with ENGO activist, July 30, 2009).

On 5 August 2008, GEP and six subsidiary companies applied for an IPO on the Shanghai Stock Exchange. The MEP placed a public notice (*gongshi*) on its website announcing the application (MEP 2008). It stated that although the seven companies "basically met" the necessary environmental conditions required for listing approval, a nine-day public comment period had been opened (MEP 2008). After learning about the public notice period from the MEP's website (Interview with ENGO activist, July 20, 2009), FON, Global Village Beijing, Green Earth Volunteers, Green Watershed, Green SOS and Greenpeace China attempted to block the IPO, based on GEP's allegedly woeful environmental record. On 12 August the six ENGOs wrote to the MEP, claiming that GEP had violated environmental laws and regulations, and should therefore be prevented from conducting its IPO (Friends of Nature 2008a). The ENGOs also claimed that GEP and its subsidiaries had violated the MEID. The ENGOs claimed that GEP and its subsidiaries, having been publicly identified by local environmental authorities for contravening environmental regulations, had ignored MEID stipulations that such "named and shamed" companies should publicly disclose environmental information within 30 days. ENGOs wrote to APP China and requested it to disclose the relevant information (Friends of Nature 2008b). Although the ENGOs received no direct response, APP issued a statement the following day defending its environmental record and emphasising its contribution to the Chinese economy (APP China 2008). Several days later, the ENGOs wrote again to APP China reiterating the request that it disclose information according to law (Friends of

Nature 2008c). On 2 September, the ENGOs wrote to the MEP and provided more details about the environmental record of Hainan Jinhai Pulp, one of the six subsidiaries (Friends of Nature 2008d). ENGOs listed 26 separate environmental violations that the company had allegedly committed within 36 months prior to its listing application. This information was in the public domain, largely thanks to an increase in information disclosure by environmental authorities in recent years (Interview with ENGO activist, July 30, 2009).

ENGO participants considered the campaign a partial success, as the IPO was delayed for nine months and the companies had to reapply (Interview with ENGO activists, July 13 & 30, 2009). ENGOs welcomed the opportunity to conduct environmental oversight of an IPO process for the first time (Interview with ENGO activists, July 13 & 30, 2009). In addition to pressuring APP China to defend its record to the Chinese public through the media, the attention led to company representatives holding a meeting with ENGO activists (Interview with ENGO activists, July 13 & 30, 2009). Even though the MEP had approved the initial IPO application from an environmental perspective, it apparently welcomed the ENGO interventions. According to an ENGO participant, the MEP benefited by raising its profile within the IPO process and showing that its regulations are effective (Interview with ENGO activist, July 13, 2009). However, the MEP eventually approved the IPO application; despite the seven companies not meeting ENGOs' information disclosure demands. In addition, one participant in the case claimed that the nine-month delay was not necessarily detrimental to GEP, due to the onset of the global financial crisis (Interview, ENGO activist, July 3, 2012).

Although ENGO activists involved in the Yuanmingyuan and GEP cases viewed their participation as beneficial in promoting the public supervision mechanism (Interview, ENGO founder, June 20, 2012), the final substantive outcomes were disappointing. In contrast, so-called NIMBY activists are primarily motivated by substantive outcomes, namely whether or not an unwanted facility is constructed in their neighbourhoods. Although NIMBY activists have engaged with the public supervision mechanism, "good governance" is seen as a means to an end rather than an end in itself (Johnson 2010). Compared with ENGOs, NIMBY activists are not easily placated by procedural good governance if they perceive outcomes as unfavourable. This can result in unintended consequences whereby NIMBYs use the public supervision mechanism to sustain and legitimise confrontations with elites based on the latter's "bad governance."

NIMBY Activism

The term NIMBY is often used pejoratively to describe selfish, irrational opposition by individuals or communities to the locating of facilities necessary for the public good such as waste incinerators or prisons in their "backyards." In some cases NIMBY activism is symptomatic of concern about potential environmental and health threats from projects such as factories and waste treatment facilities, although it can also be motivated by concern over property prices. This section discusses several high-profile NIMBY cases, drawing on documentary data and interviews with non-state participants conducted between 2009 and 2012. The cases examined involve urban, predominantly middle-class communities. They are not representative, but highlight how NIMBY actors have interacted with the public supervision mechanism. Although campaigners in these cases demonstrated strong opposition to unwanted local projects, they also displayed a desire to avoid antagonising the government, and stay within the law as far as possible. By calling for greater attention to good governance principles within the existing political system, NIMBY activists have attempted to promote society-led accountability that goes beyond the limited state-led accountability contained in the public supervision mechanism.

Despite the existence of public participation and transparency requirements, local officials are often reluctant to encourage public supervision over new, potentially lucrative, projects. An MEP official stated that from the perspective of local officials, "one fewer matter is preferable to one more matter ... Truly meaningful public participation is very rare, [officials] go through the motions, they treat public participation as a mere formality" (Interview with MEP official, June 21, 2012). This often results in projects being approved without the knowledge, let alone input, of local communities. In response to these "bad governance" practices, NIMBY actors have sometimes employed the "good governance" rhetoric stemming from the MEP's public supervision mechanism. In particular, they have strongly lamented the governments' failure to incorporate public opinion into the decision-making process as a violation of their public participation "rights" as set out by the public supervision mechanism.

In some cases, NIMBY activists have invoked the letter of the public supervision mechanism in complaining that their participatory rights have been violated. Complaints that public consultation requirements have not been adhered to can be, in the words of one environmental lawyer, a useful "entry point" (*qieru dian*) for campaigners challenging siting decisions (Interview with environmental lawyer, November 29, 2010). As well as enabling campaigners to make claims within the law, it also enables them to portray LULUs as contrary to public opinion. In this sense, public participation legislation has influenced, and opened political opportunity structures for, public mobilisation against LULUs. For example, in 2007, residents in Shanghai mobilised against the planned extension of the city's Maglev train system and demanded that a public hearing be held, as provided for by the EIA Law. They also tried to extend the boundaries of the law by asking for a longer public comment period and demanding to see the full version of the EIA report, despite the fact that legislation only requires publication of an abridged version (*The Beijing News*, January 22, 2008). Campaigners opposed to the construction of incinerators in Beijing's Liulitun and Gaoantun also complained that proper public consultation procedures had not been followed. In the former case, residents claimed that results from a questionnaire conducted as part of the EIA process were "fake" (*jia de*) (Interview with Liulitun residents, July 29, 2009). They also complained that the 100 questionnaires distributed were insufficient to gauge public opinion (Interview with Liulitun residents, July 29, 2009), despite technically meeting legislative public consultation requirements. In response, local residents conducted their own survey of 400 people, which found almost unanimous opposition to the incinerator. This highlighted the perceived gap between the siting decision and public opinion, which according to the EIA Law "should" be factored into this type of project.

SEPA itself has also faced pressure over limited transparency and for failing to consider public opinion. For example, SEPA approved the EIA for the Gaoantun incinerator in 2004.[5] Local residents challenged this decision, based partly on limited public participation, but encountered obstacles. The abridged EIA report was not released publicly, and although residents were allowed to view the report at SEPA offices, they were refused permission to photocopy or photograph it (Interview with environmental lawyer, June 22, 2012). Campaigners asked to see the contents page of the full EIA in order to determine whether or not potential health impacts had been addressed, but were refused on grounds that it would infringe on company secrets (Friends of Nature 2011). Similarly to Liulitun, the public opinion section of the EIA report also indicated public support. Yet local residents discovered through the abridged EIA report that only 50 people had been consulted via questionnaires. They subsequently filed an administrative review application with SEPA against its decision to approve the EIA, claiming it had "violated public participation principles [and] did not solicit the opinions of interested parties consistent with procedures contained in the EIA and AL laws" (Home Defence Action Group 2008). SEPA upheld its original decision, and local residents lost their appeal to the Legislative Affairs Office of the State Council. One SEPA official reportedly told campaigners that, in relation to soliciting public opinion via questionnaires, "even if we do only one [questionnaire] it means we've done it (fulfilled public consultation requirements), there are no requirements about the number [of questionnaires]" (Friends of Nature 2011). This highlights the problems that arise in relation to implementing the top-down public supervision mechanism, when officials are essentially asked to hold themselves open to public scrutiny.

NIMBY campaigners tend to use a variety of tactics in defending their interests, including protests against unwanted projects. In some cases, this leads to projects being suspended pending further inquiry and public consultation. From the government's perspective, the tactic of suspending projects pending further public consultation can buy time for the authorities, and can temporarily defuse social unrest. For example, in 2007 a reported 8,000 residents marched on government headquarters in Xiamen to express opposition to a paraxylene (PX) chemical plant that was to be constructed in the city. In response, local officials halted the project pending further investigations including public consultation. During this period the public was invited to submit comments, and the local government even convened a two-day public hearing. Although it is likely that this did not influence the final decision (Johnson 2010), arguably it reinforced the idea that the public plays a role in siting decisions. Some media reports subsequently framed the Xiamen PX case as a "win-win" situation, in that protestors behaved "rationally" and the government listened to, rather than ignored popular opinion (*People's Daily*, January 2, 2008). Similarly, a protest by Liulitun residents resulted in the incinerator being suspended. Here, as in Gaoantun and Shanghai where protests also occurred, officials convened several meetings with resident representatives. Although these meetings appear to have been rather ad hoc and informal, they enabled government officials and residents to exchange views. This was a significant improvement compared to the previous practice.

Paradoxically, although they have campaigned for their participatory rights to be upheld, citizens tend to be highly sceptical of formal channels. Unlike ENGOs, which have a long-term stake in improved legal channels for transparency and public participation, NIMBY activists exhibited significant distrust of these mechanisms, which they see as open to manipulation by decision-makers (Interview with Liulitun residents, July 29, 2009; interview with Panyu residents, July 20, 2012). As one campaigner from Guangzhou stated, regarding a public consultation exercise following the suspension of an incinerator project in the city's Panyu district,

> government departments just give us a mailbox, a fax, a phone number to allow us to express our opinions. We hope that every opinion expressed by a member of the public can be laid out under the sun so that everybody can see it, and not placed into a black hole where only … [officials] know about it" (Dayoo.com, April 13, 2011).

One problem is that officials can operate top-down participatory channels with little or no external accountability mechanisms. Despite these shortcomings in the public supervision mechanism, employing the language of good governance helps legitimise opposition to projects that have clearly violated the letter, or sometimes the spirit, of the law. Here, there are clear parallels with O'Brien and Li's "rightful resisters," who call out unruly local officials for failing to implement central-level policies (O'Brien and Li 2006). NIMBY activists have sometimes appropriated the public supervision mechanism to their own advantage by exposing cases where public opinion has not been consulted adequately. They utilise good governance principles in an instrumental way to legitimise their cause and achieve their own ends, namely the cancellation of LULUs irrespective of whether or not due process has been carried out. In this sense, the NIMBY opposition examined above has not been channelled through the public supervision mechanism; rather, the MEP's good governance agenda has provided a legitimising narrative for citizen activists who are willing to engage with formal participatory channels alongside more overt forms of protest beyond the official "good governance" institutions.

Conclusion

China's leaders have introduced good governance principles from the top-down in order to improve governance effectiveness and bolster regime legitimacy. Certain reformist officials within the MEP used this to create legal mechanisms for public participation and information disclosure. This "public supervision mechanism" was created in the hope that public involvement could improve local officials' adherence to environmental protection legislation and check powerful economic interests, which would in turn serve the MEP's interests. In other words, from its inception good governance principles and institutions were established not for their own sake, but as a means to achieve a more traditional objective of the central government, namely control of its local agents. ENGO and NIMBY activists have utilised newly established legal channels for public participation, and have demanded that good governance principles are adhered to when local officials and/or enterprises engage in what could be described as "bad governance." The MEP's good governance agenda has altered the parameters for Chinese environmental civil society by directing activism towards the public supervision mechanism and legitimising public calls for good governance principles to be enforced.

However, achieving good governance objectives in environmental protection is a difficult and contested process in China. Thus far, the public supervision mechanism has only placed a thin veneer of good governance onto an otherwise opaque and non-participatory political system with weak accountability and rule of law. Many government officials are reluctant to apply good governance principles that could reduce their control over decisions. In each of the NIMBY cases reviewed in this paper, for example, officials initially attempted to push through unwelcome projects without transparency or mean-ingful public consultation. Consequently, the public has to fight for the right to participate in planning decisions. In these NIMBY cases, officials paid greater attention to public opinion only after public unrest occurred. Yet even when public participation channels are opened, there is no guarantee that public comment will influence decisions, and officials remain reluctant to release information.

Despite the difficulties in implementation, the MEP's good governance agenda has arguably contributed to a gradual transition to a managed "Chinese" version of good governance. Pan Yue encapsulated the MEP's incremental approach to environmental governance reform when he said that "to move the system forward, we're playing a kind of game: we enforce a new environmental law – and the other side retreats a bit, and we advance a bit" (*Southern Weekend*, January 23, 2007). Civil society plays a crucial role in this process, as an ally of MEP alongside the latter's "game" to induce the compliance of local government actors, through providing external oversight and by framing demands in such a way as to invoke the good governance principles to which the central government states that it subscribes.

The cases examined in this paper do suggest, however, that although the MEP sees benefit in public supervision, it also wants this supervision to occur on its own terms. The side-lining of Pan Yue around late 2007, apparently due in part to his outspokenness on issues such as public participation and transparency, suggests disagreement within the MEP about the public's role in environmental protection (*The Guardian*, March 12, 2009). Despite this, the "good governance" agenda has endured and spread, largely due to citizen pressure. NIMBY actors, who, in common with ENGOs, have attempted to appropriate the public supervision mechanism to their own advantage, have played a key role in pushing concerns about good governance to the forefront and promoting official accountability from the bottom up. Rather than being satisfied with essentially tokenistic participation and other "due process" values in themselves, as some ENGOs appear to be, NIMBY actors are very much focused on the *substantive* ends, regardless of how they are achieved. NIMBY activists are generally loath to challenge the party-state and invite oppression upon themselves, but nor are they "embedded" within the state in the same way that some ENGOs are. NIMBY actors have thus adopted, generally, a wider variety of tactics, including highly visible protests that are symptomatic of a much more contentious approach than ENGOs. Even without any legal framework for public participation, it is likely that these citizens would mobilise against the LULUs in question. However, adopting the language of "rights," which is part of the officially mandated mechanism of public supervision, enables these actors to frame their opposition in more legitimate ways. This in turn supports persistent, sustained mobilisation and makes it harder for officials to dismiss their claims as irrational and selfish. As China's urban middle classes become increasingly aware of the negative impacts, including public health risks, associated with China's rapid modernisation, it is likely that they will follow the example of other campaigners in pressing for good governance criteria to be upheld. The ongoing legitimacy of the CCP may depend on its ability to accommodate these demands.

Acknowledgement

I would like the thank Linda Li and the anonymous reviewers for their comments. Any remaining errors are, of course, my own.

Notes

[1] SEPA was replaced by the higher-ranking MEP in 2008.
[2] Constructors who fail to carry out an EIA are allowed to do a "make-up" EIA after construction is underway. This is seen as a major weakness in the EIA process, as it effectively undermines the whole logic behind the EIA process.
[3] The Temporary Measures on Public Participation in EIA were not formally promulgated until 2006.

[4] The Nu River hydropower project was temporarily suspended in 2003 by Premier Wen Jiabao.
[5] In contrast, the Liulitun EIA had been approved by the Beijing Environmental Protection Bureau.

References

ACEF. 2008. "*2008 Zhongguo Huanbao Minjian Zuzhi Fazhan Zhuangkuang Baogao (2008 Report on the Development of China's Environmental NGOs)*." Accessed on 2 February 2009. http://www.afec.com.cn/diaocha/.

APP China. 2008. "APP (Zhongguo) Guanyu Jin Dong Zhiye (Jiangsu) Gufen Youxian Gongsi Shangshi Huanbao Hecha De Shengming (APP (China) Statement Regarding the Listing Application Environmental Protection Check of Gold East Paper (Jiangsu) Stock Company Limited)." Accessed on 15 January 2009. http://www.fon.org.cn/content.php?aid=10089.

Asian Development Bank. 1995. *Governance: Sound Development Management*. Manila: Asian Development Bank.

Cammack, P. 2004. "What the World Bank Means by Poverty Reduction, and Why It Matters." *New Political Economy* 9 (2): 189–211.

Cornwall, C., and K. Brock. 2005. "What Do Buzzwords Do for Development Policy? a Critical Look at 'Participation,' 'Empowerment' and 'Poverty Reduction'." *Third World Quarterly* 26 (7): 1043–1060.

Economy, E. 2005. "Environmental Enforcement in China." In *China's Environment and the Challenge of Sustainable Development*, edited by K. Day, 102–120. Armonk: M.E. Sharpe.

Friends of Nature. 2005. "Zhichi Zhengfu Zhendui Yuanmingyuan Pushe Fangshen Mo Shijian Juxing Tingzheng Hui De Shengming (Announcement in Support of the Government Convening a Public Hearing with Regards the Laying of Leak Prevention Material Incident at Yuanmingyuan)." Accessed on 14 January 2007. http://www.greenbeijing.net/envirinfo/ShowArticle.asp?ArticleID=990.

Friends of Nature. 2006. "2005 Nian 7 Yue 14 Ri 'Yuanmingyuan Shengtai Yu Yizhi Baohu Di Er Ci Huiyi' Fayan Jilu (14 July 2005 'Second Yuanmingyuan Ecology and Heritage Protection Meeting' Transcript)." Accessed on 15 July 2006. http://www.fon.org.cn/content.php?aid=369.

Friends of Nature. 2008a. "Duo Jia Huanbao Zuzhi Zhi Guojia Huanbao Bu De Lianmingxin: Jianyi Jinshen Chuli Bing Kaolü Zanhuan Pizhun Jindong Zhiye Shangshi Huanbao Hecha (Jointly Written Letter by Several Environmental NGOs Sent to the MEP: We Suggest that you Carefully Handle and Consider Temporarily Suspending Approval for Gold East Paper's Listing Application Environmental Protection Check)." Accessed on 14 January 2009. http://www.fon.org.cn/content.php?aid=10074.

Friends of Nature. 2008b. "NGO Zhi Jinguang Jituan Zongcai Huang Zhi Yuan Han (The Original Letter Sent by NGOs to Huang Zhi, the Chief Executive of APP)." Accessed on 14 January 2009. http://www.fon.org.cn/content.php?aid=10090.

Friends of Nature. 2008c. "Huanbao Zuzhi Zaici Yaoqiu Jindong Zhiye Dui Huanbao Hecha Neirong Jinxing Xinxi Gongkai. Huifu: APP (Zhongguo) Guanyu Jin Dong Zhiye (Jiangsu) Gufen Youxian Gongsi Shangshi Huanbao Hecha De Shengming (Environmental NGOs Once Again Request that Gold East Paper Conducts Information Disclosure in Relation to Environmental Protection Check. Response to: APP (China) Statement Regarding the Listing Application Environmental Protection Check of Gold East Paper (Jiangsu) Stock Company Limited)." Accessed on 14 January 2009. http://www.fon.org.cn/content.php?aid=10090.

Friends of Nature. 2008d. "Duo Jia Huanbao Zuzhi Zaici Zhihan Huanbao Bu: Qingqiu Huanbao Bu Zeling Jin Dong Zhiye Hecha Fanwei Nei Qiye Yansu Zhenggai Bing Zanhuan Pizhun Shangshi Huanbao Hecha (Several Environmental Protection NGOs Once Again Write a Letter to the MEP: We Request that the MEP Order Companies Included in the Gold East Paper Examination and Approval to Strictly Reform and Suspend Approval for the Listing Application Environmental Protection Check)." Accessed on 14 January 2009. http://www.fon.org.cn/content.php?aid=10140.

Friends of Nature. 2011. "Beijing Shimin Yangzi: Huanbao Bu Cheng Gaoantun Laji Fenshao Chang De Huanping Baogao Mulu Shi Shangye Jimi (Beijing Resident Yangzi: The MEP Said That the Gaoantun EIA Table of Contents Was a Trade Secret)." Presentation delivered at the 3rd Anniversary of Information Disclosure Seminar. Accessed on 14 August 2012. http://blog.sina.com.cn/s/blog_69a4de060100rurd.html.

Heberer, T., and G. Schubert 2006. "Political Reform and Regime Legitimacy in Contemporary China." *ASIEN* 99: 9–28.

Ho, P., and R. Edmonds 2007. "Perspectives of Time and Change: Rethinking Embedded Environmental Activism in China." *China Information* 21: 331–344.

Home Defence Action Group. 2008. "Gaoantun shenghuo laji fenshao chang xingzheng fuyi zhi lu (The road to administrative review for the Gaoantun domestic waste incinerator)." Accessed on 7 December 2010. http://yuedulaiyin.soufun.com/bbs/1010036393~-1~5701/77163886_77163886_%7Bpage%7D.htm.

Jahiel, A. 1997. "The Contradictory Impact of Reform on Environmental Protection in China." *The China Quarterly* 149: 81–103.

Jayasuriya, K., and K. Hewison 2004. "The Antipolitics of Good Governance: From Global Social Policy to a Global Populism?." *Critical Asian Studies* 36 (4): 571–590.

Johnson, T. 2010. "Environmentalism and NIMBYism in China: Promoting a Rules-Based Approach to Public Participation." *Environmental Politics* 19 (3): 430–448.

Ma, J. 2006. "A Path to Environmental Harmony," *China Dialogue.* Accessed on 3 October 2009. http://www.chinadialogue.net/article/show/single/en/589.

Ma, J. 2012. "The Rise of Social Accountability in China." *Australian Journal of Public Administration* 71 (2): 111–121.

MEP. 2008. "Guanyu Dui Jin Dong Zhiye (Jiangsu) Gufen Youxian Gongsi Shangshi Huanbao Hecha Qingkuang De Gongshi (Public Notice for the Environmental Protection Investigation Situation Regarding the Listing of APP (Jiangsu) Company Limited)." Accessed 13 January 2009. http://www.zhb.gov.cn/cont/gywrfz/hbhc/gsqk/200808/t20080805_126950.htm.

Mercer, C. 2003. "Performing Partnership: Civil Society and the Illusions of Good Governance in Tanzania." *Political Geography* 22: 741–763.

Mertha, A. 2008. *China's Water Warriors: Citizen Action and Policy Change.* Ithaca: Cornell University Press.

Mol, A., and N. Carter 2006. "China's Environmental Governance in Transition." *Environmental Politics* 15 (2): 149–170.

Moore, A., and A. Warren 2006. "Legal Advocacy in Environmental Public Participation in China: Raising the Stakes and Strengthening Stakeholders." *China Environmental Series* 8: 3–23.

Nanda, V. 2006. "The "Good Governance" Concept Revisited." *The ANNALS of the American Academy of Political and Social Science* 603: 269–282.

O'Brien, K., and L. Li 2006. *Rightful Resistance in Rural China.* Cambridge: Cambridge University Press.

Pan, Y. 2004. "Pan Yue: Huanjing Baohu Yu Gongzhong Canyu (Pan Yue: Environmental Protection and Public Participation)," *China Environment Online*, June 1. Accessed on 9 May 2011. http://www.china.com.cn/chinese/MATERIAL/576730.htm.

Pieke, F. 2012. "The Communist Party and Social Management in China." *China Information* 26 (2): 149–165.

Qie, J. 2011. "Huanping baogao shenpi bei zhi liuyu xingshi. Gongzhong canyu zouguochang (Approval of EIA reports claimed to tend towards formality. Public participation goes through the motions)," *Legal Daily*, September 21. Accessed on 29 August 2012. http://www.chinanews.com/ny/2011/09-21/3342783.shtml.

SEPA. 2003. "Guanyu Dui Shenqing Shangshi De Qiye He Shenqing Zai Rongzi De Shangshi Qiye Jinxing Huanjing Baohu Hecha De Tongzhi (Notice Regarding the Carrying Out of Environmental Protection Checks by Companies Applying to be Listed and by Listed Companies Applying for Refinancing)." Accessed on 29 June 2010. http://www.mep.gov.cn/info/gw/huangfa/200306/t20030616_85622.htm.

Sibbel, L. 2005. *Good Governance and Indigenous Peoples in Asia.* London: Minority Rights Group International.

State Council. 2005. *Guowuyuan Guanyu Luoshi Kexue Fazhan Guan Jia Qiang Huanjing Baohu De Jueding (State Council Decision Regarding Implementing the Scientific Development Concept and Strengthening Environmental Protection).* Accessed on 9 May 2011. http://www.gov.cn/gongbao/content/2006/content _169993.htm.

State Council. 2007. *Zhonghua Renmin Gonghe Guo Zhengfu Xinxi Gongkai Tiaoli (People's Republic of China Government Information Disclosure Ordinance).* Accessed 15 March 2009. http://www.gov.cn/zwgk/2007-04/24/content_592937.htm, State Council Order No. 492.

Van Rooij, B. 2006. "Implementation of Chinese Environmental Law: Regular Enforcement and Political Campaigns." *Development and Change* 37 (1): 57–74.

World Bank 1992. *Governance and Development.* Washington, DC: The World Bank.

Xue, L., and K. Liou 2012. "Government Reform in China: Concepts and Reform Cases." *Review of Public Personnel Administration* 32 (2): 115–133.

Young, N. 2005. "Public Enquiries Draw SEPA and Green NGOs Closer Together." *China Development Brief.* Accessed on 6 May 2007. http://www.chinadevelopmentbrief.com/node/72/print.

Yu, K. 2006. "Shehui Gongping He Shanzhi Shi Jianshe Hexie Shehui De Jishi (Social Justice and Good Governance are the Bedrock for Constructing a Harmonious Society)." *Guangming Daily.* Accessed on 24 July 2008. http://www.bjpopss.gov.cn/bjpssweb/show.aspx?id=10430&cid=48.

Zhang, W. 2006. "Long-Term Outlook for China's Political Reform." *Asia Europe Journal* 2: 151–175.

Zhang, W. 2007. "Hexie Shehui Zhi Ben: Shanzhi Yu Gongmin Shehui (The Root of Harmonious Society – Good Governance and Civil Society)." *Economic Magazine*. Accessed on 14 August 2008. http://finance.sina.com.cn/review/20070320/11493423144.shtml.

Zheng, Y. 2006. "China's Political Transition." The University of Nottingham China Policy Institute Briefing Series, Issue 14, 13 November.

Zhong, L., and A. Mol 2008. "Participatory Environmental Governance in China: Public Hearings on Urban Water Tariff Setting." *Journal of Environmental Management* 88 (4): 899–913.

Governance, Courts and Politics in Asia

BJÖRN DRESSEL

Crawford School of Public Policy, ANU, Building 132, ACT, Australia

ABSTRACT *It is widely argued that an empowered judiciary supports better governance by strengthening the rule of law and helping to make government more accountable and stable, but how solidly that reasoning is based in fact has not been carefully analysed. As recent events in Asia illustrate, apparently similar constitutional choices about courts can have very different effects on political life and ultimately governance. To address the relative lack of empirical observation and more closely investigate the nexus between courts and governance, this article first presents a basic typology of judicial politics and then applies it to Thailand, Singapore, Korea and Japan. The intent is to: (1) provide a much-needed and more nuanced view of the unfolding judicialisation phenomenon; and (2) urge closer attention to how specific patterns of judicial behaviour in Asia relate to dimensions of governance. The study thus offers an opportunity to illuminate larger issues at the intersection of judicial engagement and political governance and to advance a theoretical understanding of both.*

Over the last two decades, courts have become major players in Asian politics. No longer can the regular intervention of the Philippine Supreme Court in that country's deadlocked politics be considered unusual in the region. In Korea and Indonesia, new constitutional courts have been playing increasingly active roles. In 2004 the Korean court resolved the political stand-off that gripped Korea over the presidency of Roh Moo-hyun in 2004; and in a series of decisions in 2009 the Indonesian court cleared the path for competitive and stable presidential and parliamentary elections in 2009. In recent years, the Malaysian High Court, too, has become embroiled in several politically charged cases, and since 2006 Thailand's Constitutional Court has been issuing decisions that have drastically altered the political landscape. Even in Cambodia, Japan and Singapore, where courts have usually been quite conservative, there are hints of judicial assertiveness, though so far those courts have tended to avoid high-profile political cases.

It is possible that the trend in Asia is toward what has been called the "judicialisation of politics," which Hirschl (2006, 721) describes as "the ever-accelerating reliance on courts and judicial means for addressing core moral predicaments, public policy questions, and political controversies." But is that actually what is happening in the region? The phenomenon has been well-documented for the United States, Europe and Latin America (see, for example Sieder, Schjolden, and Angell 2005; Tate and Vallinder

1995; Stone Sweet 2000; Feeley and Rubin 1998). However, little note has been taken of its emergence in Asia (see Dressel 2012; Harding and Nicholson 2010; Ginsburg and Chen 2009). This may be because the region is still battling with legacies of executive dominance, weak rule of law and an unusual degree of regime diversity, all of which have higher visibility than what is happening in the courts. The regime diversity in fact prompted a leading scholar to claim almost 20 years ago that "a majority of Southeast Asian countries are unlikely candidates for the judicialisation of politics" because so many regimes were neither democratic nor constitutional (Tate 1994, 188).

But much has changed since Tate offered his opinion. As political and economic liberalisation have advanced (though hardly in a linear fashion and with many throwbacks), politicians and thought leaders in many countries have become more concerned both about the rule of law and about accountability and rights issues. Indeed, promoting the rule of law has gained considerable traction as new democracies emerging from authoritarian rule initiate reforms to consolidate recent democratic gains and enhance the quality of their democracy. Even less than liberal regimes have chosen constitutional reform in order to tighten social control, enhance legitimacy and ensure credible policy outcomes (see Ginsburg and Moustafa 2008). In each case, regional discourse about what constitutes good governance has reinforced the trend. As a result, in many countries, courts have to an unprecedented degree become central to political life, eliciting the inference that the region is becoming judicialised (Dowdle 2009).

But how does this new trend of judicialisation affect governance? The weight of scholarly opinion seems to be that empowered courts have a positive influence on governance: The judicial branch is critical to upholding the rule of law, for instance by protecting basic rights and freedoms and ensuring that the commitments of state actors in areas like property rights are credible; the courts, it is assumed, also provide stability and security for citizens when their interpretation and enforcement of the laws mitigates societal conflict. Courts are thought to hold government actors accountable under the law and provide checks and balances within the political process, thus making government not only more responsive but also more legitimate. In short, often against the backdrop of rule of law reforms, which are seen as necessary for the development of the market economy, democratisation and better governance, the common orthodoxy states that the judiciary – and more broadly judicialisation – are critical not only to economic development but also to "good" governance (see Harding and Nicholson 2010, 3; Golub 2003, 5).

Yet a closer look at developments in Asia raises questions about these common assumptions. There, growing judicial activism – ostensibly to promote the rule of law and make government more accountable, responsive and stable – has had, at best, ambiguous effects. Some courts have actively intervened in politics to promote good governance by providing checks and balances on executive abuse, upholding the supremacy of law and protecting the rights of citizens. Others have actively subverted the rule of law and undermined mechanisms of accountability on behalf of narrow interests or have lent support to rule *by* law. Still others have been restrained in engaging with core issues of political governance, provoking questions about their own autonomy.

These dramatic variations in judicial behaviour raise both empirical and theoretical questions about the nexus between judicialisation and governance – most obviously, why would judicial politics take such different tracks? And how is the judicialisation trend actually affecting governance? Specifically, to what extent and under what conditions does expanding judicialisation (and thus growing judicial empowerment and assertive-ness) improve prospects for the rule of law and more accountability to society, and when does it lead to more political interference in courts and even reinforce tendencies to the illiberal and arbitrary use of law?

To begin answering such questions, this paper proposes a basic typology of judicial politics and then illustrates it through a set of instructive cases from the region. The emphasis here is on "mega-politics" – the involvement of constitutional or supreme courts in particular in matters of utmost political significance (see Hirschl 2008a). That brings into focus the nexus between judicialisation and core aspects of governance. Exploring the cases through the lens of this framework, the paper advances the argument that rather than viewing judicialisation (and thus court empowerment) as positive or negative for govern-ance, it is nuances within the trend – particularly the type of judicial behaviour exhibited – that ultimately matters for aspects of governance, including such dimensions of good governance as enhanced accountability, transparency and rule-boundness.

Highlighting the different paths the phenomenon has taken and drawing closer attention to variations in the way courts in the region operate, the paper seeks to (1) provide a more empirically grounded and refined view of how the judicialisation trend has been unfolding in Asia; and (2) draw attention to the specific conditions – judicial patterns – through which courts come to influence governance. Both aspects are not only at the heart of academic debates about judicial politics but also address practical concerns related to strengthening democracy and rule of law reform.

The paper is structured as follows: First the paper briefly surveys the literature to identify basic concepts and debates, from which we derive a basic typology of judicial politics. To explore this typology empirical evidence is provided to delineate within the region critical trajectories of judicial political involvement and the impact on governance. Finally, the paper discusses what the nexus between judicialisation and governance means for both theoretical debates and practical concerns with rule of law reform and more effective courts.

Judicialisation and Governance

One aspect of judicialisation that deserves particular attention is the process by which rulings and modes of court reasoning come to influence the governance decisions of non-judicial agents (Stone Sweet 1999). Broadly defined, governance describes how authority is exercised in a polity through economic, political and social institutions, that is, the processes through which decisions are made and implemented (Kaufmann and Kraay 2008).[1] Both types of process thus intersect in the arena of judicial politics. Though that nexus may seem obvious, there is little agreement on how to conceptualise their engage-ment, what is driving it, and what its effects are.

A case in point is the corresponding concept of the judicialisation of politics. This has often suffered from a conceptual stretching that pulls together different, though sometimes interrelated, processes (see Hirschl 2008b). For instance, the abstract capture of social relations and popular culture by law due to the growing complexities of modern societies – a process that has been described as "juridification" (see Teubner 1987; Blichner and Molander 2008) – deserves thoughtful separation from the more concrete and much analysed expansion of the courts into public policy as part of "ordinary" constitutional rights jurisprudence (positive rights, procedural justice) and the redrawing of boundaries between state organs (separation of powers, federalism). Another area that is particularly relevant here is the even narrower though highly salient reliance on courts and judges for dealing with "mega-politics" – core political controversies and deep moral dilemmas related to such purely political areas as executive branch prerogatives, electoral politics and regime change (Hirschl 2008a, 99–100).

In short, essentially two notions of the judicialisation of politics can be identified. Narrowly, the term refers to the way that judges in exercising judicial review contribute to or at least influence public policy – the process by which courts, especially constitutional or supreme courts, come to dominate policy-making that previously had been the prerogative of legislatures and executives (Sieder, Schjolden, and Angell 2005; Tate and Vallinder 1995). More broadly, though, judicialisation is not limited to expansion of the scope of "judge-made law"; it also encompasses the increased presence of judicial processes and court rulings in political and social life, for instance, when social actors use the courts to advance their own interests political actors become more attuned to court actions, and state legitimacy is constructed increasingly in terms of delivering the rule of law (Domingo 2004, 108–110).

In either case judicialisation is marked by more deference to the courts, often at the expense of bureaucratic and political actors, who find themselves constrained by judicial review of administrative action or by political decision-making that is increasingly shaped by principles articulated by judges. In transforming national high courts into bodies making major political decisions, courts become active players in politics, with more influence on aspects of governance than their traditional role would allow – and politics becomes judicialised.

So far, most relevant studies have concentrated on the phenomenology of the trend and what regional and theoretical angles might be driving it. Traditionally, scholarship anchored the process at the macro-level, linking proliferation of judicial and quasi-judicial agencies to a structural transformation towards universal modernisation and democratisation that embraces the rule of law and separation of powers consistent with judicialisation from "below" or even "abroad" (Epp 1998; Guarnieri and Pederzoli 2002; Shapiro and Stone Sweet 2002; Slaughter 2000). Some studies have drawn attention to the structural dynamics and the actors involved, arguing that empowerment of courts is part of a "supply-side" process of judicialisation from "above." This can happen when self-interested strategic actors have political reasons to empower judges, such as dysfunctional institutions (Ferejohn 2002; Guarnieri and Pederzoli 2002). It may also result from attempts to avoid responsibility, in this case by shifting it to the courts (Voigt and Salzberger 2002), or to build legitimacy for contested policies (Morton 1995; Goldstein 2001). And the motivations of judges themselves should not be ignored (Bork 2003; Baum 2006). Today, two rational-strategic models dominate the discussion: an "electoral market or insurance model" (Ramseyer 1994; Ginsburg 2003) and a "hegemonic preservation model" (Hirschl 2004, 2006). Both assume that strategic elites have reasons to empower judges, whether because political parties seek "insurance" against future electoral loss or as "the by-product of a strategic interplay" among political, economic and judicial elites to insulate power arrangements against popular pressure (Hirschl 2004, 43).

Not surprisingly, the different theories about its drivers have also generated a variety of views about how the trend affects governance. For instance, scholars in the macro-level tradition often enthusiastically embrace the rise of constitutionalism globally and extol expanded judicial review as better protecting citizens and deepening democracy

(Ackerman 1997; Dworkin 1990). Ginsburg (2003, 73) sees the growing role of the judiciary as deepening democratic governance by transforming political conflict into constitutional dialogue, providing a non-partisan forum for grievances, and expressing fundamental democratic values. Others have been sceptical of the governance implications of the trend, decrying the "rise of unelected, unrepresentative, unaccountable committees of lawyers" (Bork 2003, 22), "court room politics [that are] authoritarian in both process and spirit" (Morton and Knopff 2000, 149) and the possibility of sliding towards "juristocracy" (Hirschl 2004).

While the debate has often been empirically weak, even normatively charged, it does highlight the complex interplay between judicial empowerment and aspects of govern-ance, such as the widely used dimensions of "good" governance like rule of law, accountability, predictability and representation (see Hilbink 2008; Gibler and Randazzo 2011). For instance, at the regime level it is relatively easy to view judicial actors and processes acting in support of the rule of law as part of a general process of legalisation, in fact their relationship to political accountability and representation is often far more complex. This is evidenced in long-standing debates about the balance between judicial guardianship of constitutional principles and majoritarian rule (the so-called counter-majoritarian dilemma) – and also about who guards the guardians (Friedman 2001; Graber 2008; Bickel 1962). Meanwhile, empirical studies of countries in transition are increasingly revealing the pitfalls surrounding a repositioned judiciary. They remind us that judicial self-assertion is hardly a linear process – judges are often deeply embedded in an ill-liberal past (Domingo 2004, 121) – and expose the danger that as judicial systems become more influential, policy-makers may also seek to influence the judiciary, an aspect of what scholars long ago described as the "politicisation" of the judiciary (Schmitt 1958).

The divergence of opinions clarifies that what is needed is a more nuanced under-standing of judicialisation, particularly if one wishes to thoroughly investigate the nexus between growing judicial engagement and aspects of governance, good and bad. That is why it can be useful to think in terms of a conceptual typology of judicial politics, which identifies patterns of judicial behaviour in engaging with mega-politics.

The judicialisation of politics is multi-dimensional and driven by a number of analytical factors. It depends to at least some degree on the structural independence of a court (institutional); the willingness of judges to intervene (behavioural); and facilitative support from political elites (structural); together these may well constitute dimensions of de facto independence. The involvement of judges in areas of politics can also be seen as a continuum from minimal to extensive involvement in "mega-politics." What emerges from these considerations is a simple typology of judicial politics with two dimensions – de facto judicial independence and engagement in "mega-politics" – which allows us to conceptually capture patterns of judicial behaviour as they are observable in Asia (see Figure 1).

A caution here: clearly, the relationship between judicial systems, law and politics is highly fluid. The degree of judicial involvement often varies greatly, not only from country to country but also within a country over time. Judicial engagement in mega-politics may affect different policy areas, institutions and regions differently; it might be temporary, perhaps because judges are propelled into the political fray in reaction to exceptional events such as a political crisis or deadlock, or because political actors respond to judicial activism with institutional changes that curb judicial powers. Judicialisation can also be reversed through processes of de-judicialisation. However, it is also clear that as institutional practices become engrained, the stable patterns of judicial

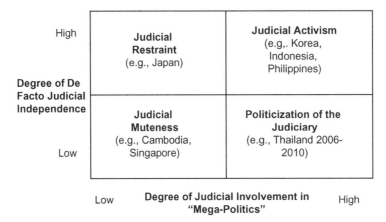

Figure 1. Typology of judicial politics.

activity that emerge allow us to characterise the behaviour of a country's courts more consistently.

The suggested typology is thus meant to bring greater analytical rigour to the study of how judicialisation affects governance by allowing for a more nuanced view of it. We can use it to identify distinct patterns of judicial politics and analyse their drivers over time (see Dressel 2012). Most importantly, we can also explore more fully how the trend affects areas of governance because the typology can be used to identify conditions in which a judicial pattern might be conducive to good governance and when it might not. For instance, does politicising the judiciary blur the lines between branches of government and undermine universal application of law, transforming judges into outright political actors with narrow interests? Or does the activism of an independent judiciary strengthen the dynamics of good governance because judges can act as veto players, societal representatives or policy-makers? Finally, when might aspects of judicial restraint (or even muteness) benefit democratic governance, and when might such a pattern work against such governance aspects as the rule of law or greater predictability and accountability?

With such questions in mind, let us turn to actual cases, partly to highlight varying nuances as the trend plays out in the region and partly to explore how such variation in court behaviour has impacted aspects of governance.

Pathways of Judicialisation in Asia

In exploring the diverse trajectories of judicialisation in Asia, we look most closely at the behaviour of Supreme or Constitutional Courts. As an instructive exercise the cases selected are countries at quite different points on the spectrum of regime types, but because their courts are most likely to be involved in mega-politics they showcase variations in the trend – and in its effects on governance.

Korea: Judicial Activism

The Korean Constitutional Court (KCC) is a good example of judicial activism in direct support of democratic governance, constitutionalism and such principles of good governance as greater accountability and representativeness. The KCC was created in 1988 as part of the political transition to Korea's Sixth Republic in 1987 (West and Yoon 1992). Since then, moving gradually beyond the quiescent institution the creators envisioned, it has become one of the most respected institutions in the country and one of the most active courts in the region (Ginsburg 2010; Yoon 2010).

Indeed, despite transitional uncertainties and occasional open political hostility, the court has regularly been called upon to resolve major political conflicts and address such political issues as electoral disputes, executive prerogatives and restorative justice. In doing so, it has carefully crafted rulings that have not only been perceived as neutral and legitimate – notwithstanding occasional harsh criticism from political and social forces – but has also expressed a consistent preference for such good governance principles as rule of law, representation and participation and accountability. The court is considered to have opened up a new era of judicialisation of politics in Korea (Park 2008).

The KCC has solid institutional structures and far-reaching powers. The bench consists of nine judges who serve renewable terms of six years. Though all nine justices are appointed by the president, with the consent of the National Assembly, in practice three are selected by the National Assembly and three nominated by the chief justice of the Supreme Court. The system allows candidates to be drawn from different professional backgrounds. Institutional safeguards of independence (budget autonomy, tenure and the like) are strong by international standards, and the court's powers extend beyond judicial review into such areas as impeachment, the constitutionality of parties, electoral politics and jurisdictional conflict between branches of government (Kim 2010). Also, under articles 68(2) of the Constitutional Court Act, there is the possibility of the court hearing private constitutional complaints. These institutional arrangements have allowed the KCC to become highly assertive and effective, which is not always true of other Korean courts. By 2011 the court had received 20,173 cases; it had invalidated or partially repudiated legislative acts in 526 cases and upheld 337 constitutional complaints.[2]

Several cases illustrate the far-reaching consequences for governance of KCC decisions. In its first decade, in a string of high-profile decisions the court struck down laws that required large registration fees for minority candidates or a higher deposit from independent than from party-affiliated candidates and that gave party-based candidates advantages over independents in campaigning and leafleting.[3] The court also rectified disproportional representation for rural and urban districts.[4] Ruling that the constitutional guarantee of equality of opportunity and the right to run for or hold office is a core democratic freedom, the court not only addressed electoral distortions, it also actively supported a more representative and competitive democratic process (Ginsburg 2003, 226–246).

In the new century the KCC has continued to intervene directly in political matters. It declared unconstitutional the levying of tax on a consolidated family basis and has championed the rights of minorities, such as women and disabled people.[5] Such much-debated decisions have forced the government to make far-reaching changes in economic and social policy (see Park 2008, 221–229). Yet the full extent of the KCC's judicial activism only became visible in 2004 with decisions in two landmark cases.

In the Relocation of the Capital City Case, the KCC declared unconstitutional a government bill to move the capital from Seoul to another area to promote equal and balanced growth.[6] The court decided that the historical acceptance of Seoul as the capital established a kind of "customary constitution" – thus in effect setting a new, unwritten, constitutional standard that allows the KCC to measure the constitutionality of legislation on core policy issues (Park 2008, 78–81). Then, the court took up the attempted impeachment of President Roh Moo-Hyun, wading into issues of political stalemate and potential political crisis.[7] Asked whether the president had violated the law by what appeared to be campaigning for his own party during contested mid-term elections, the court found grounds for several violations but rejected his removal as disproportionate – a measured approach since by the time the court ruled Roh's party had already won an overwhelming election victory (Lee 2005).

In taking on these cases, the KCC managed to become the final arbiter in politically charged cases, often at the expense of such institutions as parliament or the executive, and performed that role in subsequent cases involving Roh and his successor, President Lee Myung-bak.[8] Yet in establishing itself as an active player in the political process – one that acts decisively yet with carefully strategic consideration – the KCC has also made a positive contribution to democratic constitutional order in general, for instance ensuring fairness in the electoral process and functioning as a critical constitutional veto player (Ginsburg 2010, 149). Indeed, building on a solid foundation for independence and careful strategic respect for other branches of government, the court has helped deepen the quality of the democratic process and aspects of good governance in Korea.

Thailand: Politicisation of the Judiciary

The trajectory of the Thai Constitutional Court since 2006 has been quite different. Rather than being driven by the assertiveness of an independent judiciary, Thai judicial activism in areas of politics seems instead to reflect a general politicisation of the judiciary (Dressel 2010).

The first decade of Thailand's Constitutional Court had been tumultuous (see Klein 2003; Harding 2010). Established in 1998 as part of the 1997 "People's Constitution," the court was subjected to public criticism early on for its conservatism during the government of Prime Minister Thaksin Shinawatra (2001–06). It was then dissolved by the 2006 military coup that revoked the 1997 constitution; it was replaced by a military-appointed Constitutional Tribunal, then reconstituted by the 2007 constitution with modified structures, powers and bench. Against a background of political polarisation and intra-elite conflict that has been growing since the 1997 constitution came into force, this and other courts have increasingly intervened in areas of mega-politics, drawing accusations of, at best, a lack of impartiality, at worst, outright political bias.

Few would have predicted such a trajectory. Taking the French and German constitutional courts as models, the Thai version is in many ways similar to others in the region. Envisioned as the guardian of the new liberal architecture and a hub of a network of oversight agencies to strengthen rule-based governance, originally the court enjoyed comparatively broad jurisdiction and (at least formally) solid safeguards for its independence. Its bench, at first 15 judges, now nine, is chosen through a process that has produced a professionally diverse bench of judges each sitting for a single non-renewable term of nine years (Harding and Leyland 2011, 166–169).

The 2007 constitution explicitly and significantly politicised the court by, for instance, involving it in the selection of senators and candidates for managing the independent agencies; allowing it to propose laws directly to the House of Representatives; and, most controversially, giving it the power to dissolve a political party if one of its leaders is found guilty of election fraud (Elkins and Ginsburg 2009; Dressel 2009, 311–312).

Perhaps the first manifestation of a new judicial assertiveness was the Constitutional Court's decision to annul the April 2006 general elections.[9] The Thaksin government had decided to call snap elections to counter growing public protest about allegations of disloyalty to the monarchy, corruption and conflicts of interest; opposition parties boycotted the election. The court's decision to nullify the elections was remarkable both in itself and in how it was handled. The unusually broad reasoning of the verdict directly challenged the opinions of the Election Commission, which many experts considered valid (see Nelson 2006); there also seemed to be an unusual degree of coordination between courts: The Administrative Court had decided in April to cancel the re-run election of parliamentarians, the Constitutional Court annulled the general election and the Criminal Court brought actions against the Election Commissioners – actions that observers linked to a previous speech in which the revered monarch directly urged the judiciary to find a solution to the political impasse (Hewison 2010, 134).[10]

Then in May 2007 a Constitutional Tribunal decision dissolved the Thai Rak Thai (TRT) party and barred 111 of its members from public office for five years.[11] It was the first case heard by the military-appointed court, many of whose members had been overtly critical of the Thaksin government. The decision came only days after another royal speech to the Administrative Court in which the king urged the judges to find a solution to the political crisis, stating: "I have the answer in my heart, but have no right to say it" (*The Nation*, 25 May 2007). In finding TRT and allies Pattana Chart and Chart Thai guilty of election violations, the court effectively decapitated Thailand's largest and most popular political party, which had won landslide victories in 2001 and 2005. Not only was Thaksin now ineligible to run for office, so was virtually anyone else who had risen with him.

The same ruling unanimously acquitted the military-favoured Democrat Party of charges it faced regarding the 2006 election, despite evidence of illicit activities. Later the Supreme Court decided to seize almost US$1.7 billion in Thaksin family assets. Concerns grew that the judges were implicitly supporting the junta's agenda. Since some justices also had unusually harsh words for the former prime minister, there were grounds for the impression that the tribunal bent legal rules to achieve a politically desired outcome.

Two Constitutional Court cases in late 2008 suggested that the earlier decisions were not aberrations and added to the impression of bias against Thaksin and his parties. The first found Prime Minister Samak Sundaravej guilty of a conflict of interest (and thus breach of s. 269 of the constitution) in receiving a honorarium for appearances on a popular TV cooking show[12]; the second dissolved the People's Power Party (PPP), the political successor of the TRT.[13] Both were heard after a strong win by the PPP in junta-organised general elections in December 2007 and with a growing political stand-off between anti- and pro-Thaksin political camps. The decisions again had bold political implications: Prime Minister Samak was forced to resign for what many considered a minor abuse of power and successor Prime Minister Somchai Wongsawat also had to resign after PPP executive Yongyut Tiyapairat was found guilty of vote buying. The path was thus cleared for a Democrat Party-led government. The decisions are both notable for judicial creativity in constitutional interpretation and for breaches of procedural due process, which looked suspiciously like the *un*-rule of law.

These and other Constitutional Court decisions have profoundly altered governance in Thailand: The judges have effectively destroyed the country's largest and most successful political party, forced the resignation of two prime ministers and kept pressure on popular former Prime Minister Thaksin to remain in exile. Other courts have followed the Constitutional Court lead; both the Supreme Administrative Court and the Supreme Court have issued rulings that directly interfere with government policy.[14] Meanwhile, the elite-favoured Democrat Party has received very different treatment. The 2010 case to dissolve that party was thrown out on a technicality despite evidence of election violations similar to those of the PPP (*The Economist*, 29 November 2011).

It thus appears that the growing involvement of the courts in areas of "mega-politics" has less to do with its asserting judicial independence and more to do with its having been politicised by traditional elites (see McCargo 2005, 2008). Indeed these elites have increasingly come to rely on the courts to advance their interests and block attempts for reform. That trend has continued, though somewhat moderated, since the formation in 2011 of the Pheu Thai government under the leadership of Thaksin's sister, Yingluck Shinawatra, who has seen her principal concern – constitutional reform – thwarted by the court, which in 2012 stopped a final vote in parliament on the Constitutional Drafting Assembly Bill. However, although it accepted a complaint from the opposition that the Pheu Thai party had violated the constitutional safeguards for the "king as head of state," it declined to dissolve the party.

Yet the situation suggests that a growing judicialisation of politics carries the risk of politicising the courts as policy-makers and elites seek to influence court decisions – especially when elite divisions are widening amid uncertainties over the immanent royal succession. A number of video scandals in 2010 have shown judges discussing political cases not yet decided and leaking judicial examination papers to favoured candidates (*The Economist*, 11 November 2010). That politicisation undermines not only the professionalism of the judges and the legitimacy of the courts but also basic principles of democratic good governance, such as equitable application of the law and accountability to society, as has previously been seen in places like Cambodia and more recently the Philippines (see Cienca 2012; Un and So 2012).

Japan: Judicial Restraint

An equally instructive case, though offering a different type of lesson, is that of the Supreme Court of Japan, which despite considerable nominal independence has opted not to engage with mega-politics at all. Thus it is perhaps not surprising that although it is "among the most honest, politically independent, and professionally competent [courts] in the world today" (Haley 2007, 99), it is also considered one of the most conservative (Law 2009). Since its founding in 1947 the court has struck down only eight statutes on constitutional grounds (by contrast, the German Constitutional Court has struck down 600), and even in those cases its constitutionality rulings have been less than momentous. In cases of significant political impact it has steadfastly avoided ruling on the constitutional merits at all.

Such unusual restraint within an otherwise highly legalistic society has naturally drawn comment. Some scholars ask how independent the 15-member Supreme Court can be, considering the political dominance of the Liberal Democratic Party and its indirect means of influencing appointments and promotions (Ramseyer and Rasmusen 2003). Others found evidence of an "extraordinary record of integrity and ... political independence" even while describing the court "as by far the least influential, much less dangerous, branch of government" (Haley 2006, 5). Recent studies have argued that the court as an *institution* enjoys considerable independence, but that *individual judges* face pressures for restraint from the control exerted by the General Secretariat of the Supreme Court over selection, training and career trajectories and by the common practice of appointing judges to the court shortly before mandated retirement (Upham 2005; Law 2009).

Thus, rather than barriers being directly raised against liberal-activist judges, it is the internal organisational structure and the legal culture that have kept activism at bay (O'Brian and Ohkoshi 2001).[15] Also, it has been suggested that Supreme Court judges view the constitution as more an articulation of political principles than a source of law (Matsui 2011), or as part of a legacy of German "organ theory" in Japanese law that limits constraints on public authority through judicial review by ensuring the autonomy of each state organ (Ginsburg and Matsudaira 2012).

These debates aside, of the Supreme Court's few rulings on constitutionality, hardly any would be considered mega-political.[16] True, it has heard a string of prominent cases concerning apportionment of electoral districts, but only one had mega-political implications – the 1976 Kurokawa v. Chiba decision, which rejected a legislative scheme that weighted the votes of rural votes five times more heavily than those of urban voters.[17] However, while the court implied that the disproportion should be addressed, it did not do so itself by setting a precise allowable ratio for future cases; nor did it even void the election in question (Law 2009, 1547–1548). The court later made similar rulings even though the Diet had failed to address the situation. It is clearly reluctant to order parliament to act or to set legal boundaries on its activities.[18]

Equally important, on perhaps the most politically charged question it has faced – challenges to security arrangements under Article 9 of the post-war constitution, which prohibits maintenance of armed forces or other "war potential" – the court has steadfastly refused to rule (Law 2009, 1548). Its reasoning was expressed as early as 1959 in the Sunakawa case, when the Supreme Court overturned a lower court decision on the unconstitutionality of a special law regulating US base facilities under the 1952 Security Treaty; the court said that only "obvious" constitutional violations should be overturned, and that it should contain itself to the exercise of its "purely judicial function." It has continued to apply this approach.[19]

Reforms initiated in the 1990s to expand the role of law, and by extension that of courts, have yet to have much impact. While the courts are independent and even activists on rights issues, they are adverse to any ruling that might involve them in contested political issues, as illustrated in recent cases dealing with visits of high-ranking politicians to the Yasukuni Shrine and their possible violation of the separation of state and church; the involvement of Japan's self-defence forces in Iraq as violating Article Nine; and compensation claims by former "comfort women" and forced labourers from other Asian countries.[20] Although several high-profile cases dealing with the right of citizens living abroad to vote in elections and the disqualification of children born to a Japanese father and non-Japanese mother from acquiring citizenship have been described as "epoch-making" in taking the rights of individuals seriously, the cases were often decided on administrative rather than constitutional grounds.[21]

Japan demonstrates that judicial independence does not necessarily lead to judicial activism. In fact, for reasons of both internal organisation and legal culture, the high court may deliberately decide to exercise restraint in certain cases and thus avoid core political and social controversies. How long that position can be sustained remains to be seen, though. In Malaysia, for instance, the Supreme Court was similarly restrained from 1957 through 1988; after that, growing elite cleavages propelled the courts into the political fray. Clearly, court behaviour can change quickly in response to structural changes that affect politics and elites.

Singapore: A Muted Approach

The trajectory of the Singapore Supreme Court is clearly marked by limited judicial independence and limited engagement in mega-politics. Operating within the "soft authoritarian" rule of the People's Action Party (PAP) the court draws attention not only to the limits of judicial autonomy in settings of executive dominance but also to the complexities of judicial behaviour in such a setting with respect to areas of governance (see Rodan 2004; Worthington 2003; Rajah 2012).

Singapore's judicial and legal system is regularly ranked among the best in the world by international benchmarks, such as the World Justice Rule of Law Index and the Centre For Financial Stability Rule of Law Index, and the government has gone to great lengths to stress the role of the courts in ensuring good governance (see, for example, a speech by Lee Kuan Yew (2007) to the International Bar Association in 2007). However, over the years some serious questions have been raised about court impartiality and independence, particularly in politically sensitive cases (see, for example, Frank 1991; International Bar Association 2008; Littlemore 1998). Worthington (2001, 133) says, given PAP dominance, "separation of powers is observed in work only; the legislature and the judiciary are disenfranchised by the executive, and the legal profession has no capacity to challenge or even advise the executive." Hence, as a result of considerable government control and pervasive corporatist ideology rather than voluntary restraint, courts in Singapore have shown few signs of judicial activism and have had virtually no engagement with "mega-politics."

Since the Singapore Supreme Court was founded in 1957, it has exercised its judicial review powers cautiously, having reviewed 79 cases (27.8% of which the applicant won), and virtually none of its cases have addressed substantive constitutional or political issues. In fact, the five-year reviews of legal developments published by the Singapore Academy of Law provide not a single chapter on constitutional and administrative law, as the Chief Justice pointed out recently (Keong 2010, 473). While this partly reflects a lack of open contestation in a tightly controlled political system, it also illustrates government efforts to subtly control the judiciary, particularly the Supreme Court, through such means as removal of external review, with appeals to the Privy Council having ceased in 1994; legislation to curtail sentencing prerogatives; direct influence over the terms of appointments through exercise of executive discretion in appointing Supreme Court judges (many of whom are claimed to have links to the PAP inner circle); rotation of judges through legal service positions; lack of tenure for many judges; and extension of contracts at the Supreme Court beyond legal retirement age at the will of the prime minister (Worthington 2001, 498). These are in addition to the firm regulation of judges through corporatist control over such professional organisations as the Singapore Law Society and institutions of higher legal education – the gateways to the bench. Given the intimate ties of judges to the PAP regime and its corporatist ideology, it is not surprising that courts rarely, if ever, address core political issues.

This is not to say that the judiciary is irrelevant. The government has been careful to support the image of a professional and efficient judiciary, and the Supreme Court has done a great deal to retain the confidence of the international community in its commercial decisions. But more politically sensitive cases often reveal very different dynamics. For instance, in cases against prominent opposition members the courts have deviated from long-held principles of English law. Canadian Judge Paul Bentley, an International Commission of Jurists (ICJ) observer for the J.B. Jeyaratnam trial stated:

> The logic escapes me! [Judge] Rajendran indicated that he was adopting the reasoning of the English House of Lords in Rubber Improvements Ltd. v Daily Telegraph Ltd […] as the correct interpretation of the law of defamation […] On this reasoning, Jeyaratnam's words to the crowd could not be defamatory. Yet the conclusion of Judge Rajendran runs in clear opposition to the rationale in the Lewis' case" (cited in Worthington 2001, 491).

In defamation and contempt cases often brought against regime critics, the damages awarded have been drastically different in political and non-political cases (see Worthington 2003, 126). In fact, because the courts have been used blatantly for political purposes, there may have been difficulties in filling the Supreme Court bench, with some judges accepting appointments only on the condition that they are not involved in political cases; the bench is thus increasingly divided between "technical" and "political" judges (Worthington 2001, 516), lacking the bureaucratic autonomy of the Japanese court, and with some judges actively supporting the corporatist communal ideology that seeks to keep political conflict out of the courts. See, for example, a recent speech by Chief Justice Chan Sek Keong to law students in which he advocated a "green light approach" which views courts not as the "first line of defence against administrative abuses of power: instead, control can and should come internally from Parliament and the Executive itself…" thus leaving the role of courts to one of support in "articulating clear rules and principles by which government may abide one and conform to the rule of law" (Keong 2010, 480). On the rare occasions when the Supreme Court has engaged with areas of mega-politics (cases against opposition members) it has done so as a direct result of its instrumentalisation by the executive.

The Singaporean court demonstrates how deeply embedded courts are in such one-party political systems and the difficulty of judicial assertiveness where the executive is dominant. As can similarly be seen in socialist regimes in the region, such as China and Vietnam, the government's ability to project a public image, even if partially, of judicial impartiality and independence in non-political cases reveals the complexities of the relationship between judicialisation and governance in certain settings.

Conclusion

As the role of courts grows in Asia, this paper has drawn attention to variations within the judicialisation trend as it unfolds there, with particular reference to the area of mega-politics. In highlighting a basic typology of judicial politics and illustrating it with cases from the region, the purpose has been to question common assumptions that the relationship of an empowered judiciary to governance can only be positive. Instead, drawing attention to a more nuanced and multifaceted understanding of judicial engagement with governance, the goal is ultimately to provide new insights for theoretical and empirical debate, not only in the as yet understudied Asian context but also more globally.

A particular challenge throughout has been conceptual: Both the term "judicialisation" and the concept of "governance" (and its often normatively charged corollary of "good governance") have been open to interpretation. Recognising that, we have tried to focus tightly on the narrower but highly relevant judicialisation of "mega-politics" – in particular the critical nexus between judicial engagement and governance – while informing the study, as is done in the traditional use of good governance in the development literature, with consideration of such dimensions of governance as enhanced accountability, transparency and the rule of law. The approach has obvious limitations, but it is helpful to this paper in challenging current orthodoxy by making possible a more nuanced and complex understanding of the concept of governance and the related "good governance" discourse.

The cases presented here offer rich new insights for understanding of not only the judicialisation trend itself but also its nexus to governance. For instance, there is little doubt that at a macro level the rise of democracy and constitutional law in Asia has often been the foundation of growing judicial assertiveness and activism in core political matters. This should not be surprising. Indeed, these reforms, often directly animated by goals of better governance, have often repositioned and empowered the courts in relation to other branches of government, and almost as often have created specialised courts specifically designed to be final arbiters in constitutional and governance-related matters. But the effects of such changes are hardly clear-cut. Soft authoritarian regimes like that of Singapore have begun to see the benefits of a well-functioning and at least partially autonomous judiciary even as they set limits on the involvement of the courts in mega-politics. Elsewhere, heightened political contestation has led to politicisation of the judiciary as elites have seen the benefit of using courts for their own ends in politically charged cases.

In their diversity, the cases presented highlight the need to move beyond macro-level explanations and to investigate the complex interplay between institutional, ideational and structural factors in shaping judicial behaviour. Certainly, court powers and scope, as well as more general arrangements for enhancing judicial independence (such as tenure, budget autonomy and appointment procedures), have often triggered judicial assertiveness in political matters. Yet, as Japan illustrates, how these arrangements are nuanced might also reinforce an internal culture that makes it less likely that courts will take on a policy-making role. The legal traditions in which judges are socialised as well as trained, and the general understanding of law and state, have often provided an ideational "stickiness" that leads to serious path dependencies for judicial activity, particularly when it comes to core areas of governance, such as electoral disputes, executive prerogatives or nationally divisive constitutional matters.

Perhaps most important is the structural context itself. All the cases presented illustrate that courts cannot help but be deeply embedded within the political realm, in particular the elite dynamics, that sets the general parameters in which courts can operate. Elite dynamics not only critically determine whether courts will be propelled into the political fray but, as the cases indicate, they are also critical in shaping behaviour when courts are confronted with mega-political issues. For instance, in Korea and Indonesia, elite configurations have been diffused, allowing for societal acceptance of the courts as final arbiters; there the courts have seized on the political space to not only engage in areas of governance, but also to actively advance the good governance agenda (Dressel and Mietzner 2012). On the other hand, where elites have managed to align the courts to their purposes, as in Thailand, or shown little division amongst each other, as in Singapore, courts are unlikely to even look for room to intervene; nor are they able to actively shape a good governance agenda that might run against engrained elite interests.

The borders between the different trajectories are often fluid, responding to changes in the structural environment and the strategic behaviour of courts themselves. For instance, as the Thai court illustrates, growing judicial activism carries a danger of growing politicisation, particularly in times of acute political crisis. Similarly, a judiciary muted by executive control, as in Singapore, is at permanent risk of being instrumentalised should political elites so choose. And whether self-imposed judicial restraint despite formal independence might ultimately lead to greater activism might also be questioned, keeping in mind the case of Japan. The typology sketched out here should thus be seen as simply a starting point for analysis. But because it allows classification for comparative purposes, it can be tremendously useful for drawing inferences about the conditions and drivers of judicial behaviour and its effects.

Consider the effects of judicialisation in areas of governance. However appealing, given the variety of experiences in Asia alone, it seems that assumptions that greater judicial independence and assertiveness will necessarily lead to improvements in the rule of law, constitutional practice and the dynamics of good governance are not easily justifiable. Indeed, as our typology helps highlight, distinct patterns of judicial behaviour in areas of mega-politics can have a variety of effects on governance. For instance, there is little doubt that a judiciary lacking independence is highly problematic. Take the case of a politicised judiciary, as in Thailand between 2006 and 2010, when the courts were used to advance partisan interests and as a result undermined the equitable application of law. Not only did the court increase exclusion from the governance process for numerous popular parties, it also exacerbated political conflict. Likewise, where the judiciary is deliberately muted, as in many authoritarian and semi-authoritarian regimes, fundamental issues are raised in terms not only of protection from arbitrary action but also of participation and access to justice, which are critical to regime legitimacy.

Instances of growing judicial activism or self-imposed restraint are more difficult to evaluate. For instance, while some scholars have suggested that growing judicial assertiveness has been critical to deepening the democratic process, heightening the accountability of public officials, and making the state more responsive to individual and socioeconomic rights – particularly in transitional democratic settings like South Korea, Taiwan, and Indonesia – others have been wary of judicial involvement in policy areas and the bold expansion of judicial powers by judges themselves (for example, the "basic structure" doctrine in India or recourse to a "customary constitution" in Korea). This is partly because judicial actors lack expertise in and capacity for public policy-making and partly because there is a danger that judicial powers might expand at the expense of other institutional actors, particularly those legitimated by popular mandate. But this is not to say that judicial restraint is always the answer; it, too, carries risks, such as that contested issues of mega-politics are never resolved or are badly addressed, which reinforces uncertainty and ultimately erodes at least political stability, if not legitimacy.

Given the possibilities of such different trajectories (not to mention combinations and variations of them), what seems to emerge from different Asian case studies is the pragmatic insight that the effects of judicialisation on governance depend on both the strategic behaviour of the courts and their constitutional dialogue with other branches of government. Rather than conceptualising judicial empowerment as a zero-sum game, what matters is how meaningful dialogue on critical issues is fostered and engages all institutions, to the ultimate transformation of political conflict into constitutional politics. This is particularly true for issues of "mega-politics," which by nature are likely to be deeply divisive.

So far, courts in the region have differed about how to facilitate political dialogue and create sufficient political space for full debate. The South Korean Constitutional Court has done this largely by dismissing cases, while the Taiwanese Constitutional Court has often explicitly demanded that political actors enter into dialogue (Yeh 2010). On the same path are the Indian Supreme Court, the Indonesian Constitutional Court and the Philippines Supreme Court, all of which have sought explicitly to engage other branches of government (Cienca 2012; Mietzner 2010; Shankar 2012). Hence, as these different strategies illustrate, judicial actors are painfully aware that, as usually the weakest branch of government, they must carefully choose their battles and the scope of their interventions. This is particularly so in transitional settings, where due to fragile institutional arrangements courts are limited in how they affect social change and resolve intense political disputes. Here it may well be that courts through procedural solutions and facilitation of constitutional dialogue help deepen governance dynamics in Asia.

In sum, statements about the unfettered benefits for good governance of an empowered and assertive judiciary need to be carefully qualified in light of the country context. This is particularly true in Asia, a region that is not only host to unprecedented regime diversity but that still struggles with authoritarian enclaves, legacies of executive dominance and an often technocratic understanding of the judicial process and the rule of law. The effects of foreign transplants like constitutional courts and broad assumptions about how the rule of law is created thus need to be analysed in situ; theoretical analysis of such slippery concepts as judicialisation and governance and how they interact must be tested on the ground. What we have seen from the cases is that many of the institutional and other factors that weigh upon governance also weigh upon the courts, and influence their interaction – and the differentiated nuances matter.

Notes

[1] The concept of "governance" has been clouded by a slew of different definitions over the years. Here, for simplicity's sake, we accept the encompassing definition used in association with the World Bank governance indicators. Even more contested is the phrase "good governance," which generally encompasses such elements as participation, transparency, accountability, predictability and rule of law (for a critical review see Doornbos (2001).

[2] See the official statistics of the Constitutional Court on its website (http://english.ccourt.go.kr/home/english/decisions/stat_pop01.jsp).

[3] One-Person One-Vote Case, 13–2 KCCR 77; 2000Hun-Ma91; 2000Hun-Ma112; 2000Hun-Ma134 (Consolidated) 19 July 2001; National Assembly Members Act Case, 89 HonKa 6, 1 KCCR 199, 249 (8 September 1989); and National Assembly Members Act Case, 92 HonMa 37, 39, 4 KCCR 137 (13 March 1992).

[4] Electoral District Disproportionality Case, 95 HonMa 224, 7–2 KCCR 760 (17 December 1995).

[5] Comprehensive Real Estate Case, 2006Hun-Ba112; 2007Hun Ba 71, 88; 2008 Hun Ba3, 62; 2008Hun-Ka12 (Consolidated), 13 November 2008; and House Head System Case, 2001 Hun-Ga9; 2004 Hun-Ga5 (consolidated), 3 February 2005; Visual Handicapped Masseurs Case, 2006 Hun-Ma1098 (Consolidated), 30 October 2008.

[6] 2004 Hun-Ma554, 566 (consolidated), 21 October 2004.

[7] Impeachment of the President Case, 16–1 KCCR 609, 2004Hun-Na1 (14 May 2004).

[8] 2007 Hun-ma 1468, 10 January 2008.

[9] Constitutional Court Decision No. 9/2549 (2006).

[10] See for an unofficial translation of the king's speech, *The Nation*, 27 April 2007.

[11] Constitutional Tribunal Decision No. 3-5/2550 (2007).

[12] Constitutional Court Decision No. 12-13/2551 (2008).

[13] Constitutional Court Decision No. 20/2551 (2008).

[14] See, for instance, the Supreme Administrative Court's temporary injunction against 76 major investment projects worth Bt400bn (US$12 billion) at and around the Map Ta Phut industrial estate (Court Order 592/2552 (2009)).

[15] Widely debated exceptions were the cases against judge Fukushima, a member of the leftist Young Jurist League in the 1960s and the non-renewal of Judge Miyamoto Yasuaki in 1971.

[16] The majority of the cases have involved the court striking down: a law punishing patricide more severely than other forms of homicide (Aizawa v. Japan, 27KEISHU 265 (Sup. Ct, April 1973); a law restricting the abilities of pharmacies to operate within close physical proximity of one another (Sumiyoshi K.K. v. Governor, Hiroshima-ken, 29 MINSHU 572 (Sup. Ct, April 1975); a rule limiting the liability of the postal service for the loss of registered mail (Shichifuku Sangyo K.K. v. Japan, 56 MINSHU 1439 (Sup. Ct, 11 September 11 2002); a law restricting the co-owners of forest land to subdivide their property (Hiragushi v. Hiragushi, 41 MINSHU 408 (Sup. Ct, 22 September 1987); a statutory provision that distinguished for purposes of eligibility between illegitimate children of Japanese fathers who acknowledged paternity prior to birth and those whose fathers acknowledged paternity only subsequent to birth (Jane Doe v. Japan, 62 MINSHU 1367 (Sup. Ct, 4 June 2008).

[17] Kurokawa v. Chiba Prefecture Election Commission, 30 Minshu 223 (Sup. Ct G.B., 14 April 1976).

[18] See in particular; Kanao v. Hiroshima Election Management Commission, 39 Minshu 1100 (Sup. Ct, G.B., 17 July 1985) in which the question of a 4:1 ratio was discussed again; and the subsequent decision on the suggested 2:1 ratio following the 1994 electoral reform in: Supreme Court Grand Bench Decision of 10 November 1999, (1) 53 Minshu 8–1577, 1696 Hanji 48, Hanta 114, (2) 53 Minshu 8–1704, 1696 Hanji 46, 1018 114, which dismissed approximately 31 appeals by citizen groups from lower court decisions seeking nullification of the House of Representatives election of 20 October 1996.

[19] For the earlier case, see Sunakawa Case, 13 KEISHU 3225 (Sup. Ct, 16 December 1959). On the latter, see Naganuma Nike Missile Site Case 1982.

[20] See Yasukuni Shrine, 1940 Hanji 122 (Sup. Ct. 2nd Bench decision, 23 June 2006). For Article 9, see Nagoya High Court, 17 April 2008 (unpublished decision). The final case can be found at Nagoya High Court ruling 31 May 2007, 54 Shomu Geppo 287. The Supreme Court refused to hear the appeal (Sup. Ct decision 11 November 2008).

[21] For the former case, see 2001 (Gyo-Tsu) No. 81, 2001 (Gyo-Hi) No. 76, 2001 (Gyo Tsu) No. 83, 2001 (Gyo-Hi) No. 77, 2005. On the latter case, see 2000 (Gyo-Hi), No. 149.

References

Ackerman, B. 1997. "The Rise of World Constitutionalism." *Virginia Law Review* 83: 771–797.

Baum, L. 2006. *Judges and Their Audiences: A Perspective on Judicial Behavior.* Princeton: Princeton University Press.

Bickel, A. 1962. *The Least Dangerous Branch: The Supreme Court at the Bar of Politics.* New Haven: Yale University Press.

Blichner, L., and A. Molander. 2008. "Mapping Juridification." *European Law Journal* 14 (1): 36–54.

Bork, R. 2003. *Coercing Virtue: The Worldwide Rule of Judges.* Washington, DC: American Enterprise Institute.

Cienca, Jr., A. 2012. "From Judicialization to Politicization of the Judiciary: The Philippine Case." In *The Judicialization of Politics in Asia*, edited by B. Dressel, 117–138. London: Routledge.

Domingo, P. 2004. "Judicialization of Politics or Politicization of the Judiciary? Recent Trends in Latin America." *Democratization* 11 (1): 104–126.

Doornbos, M. 2001. "Good Governance': The Rise and Decline of a Policy Metaphor?" *Journal of Development Studies* 37 (6): 93–108.

Dowdle, M. 2009. "On the Regulatory Dynamics of Judicialization: The Promise and Perils of Exploring 'Judicialization' in East and Southeast Asia." In *Administrative Law and Governance in Asia*, edited by T. Ginsburg and A. Chen, 23–37. London: Routledge.

Dressel, B. 2009. "Thailand's Elusive Quest for a Constitutional Equilibrium, 1997–2007." *Contemporary Southeast Asia* 31 (2): 296–325.

Dressel, B. 2010. "Judicialization of Politics or Politicization of the Judiciary? Considerations From Recent Events in Thailand." *The Pacific Review* 23 (5): 671–691.

Dressel, B. ed. 2012. *The Judicialization of Politics in Asia*. London: Routledge.

Dressel, B., and M. Mietzner. 2012. "A Tale of Two Courts. The Judicialization of Electoral Politics in Asia." *Governance* 25 (3): 393–414.

Dworkin, R. 1990. *A Bill of Right for Britain*. London: Chatto and Windus.

Elkins, Z., and T. Ginsburg. 2009. "Ancillary Powers of Constitutional Courts." *Texas Law Review* 87: 1431–1461.

Epp, C. R. 1998. *The Rights Revolution: Lawyers, Activists and Supreme Courts in Comparative Perspective*. Chicago: University of Chicago Press.

Feeley, M., and E. Rubin. 1998. *Judicial Policy Making and the Modern State: How the Courts Reformed America's Prisons*. Cambridge: Cambridge University Press.

Ferejohn, J. 2002. "Judicializing Politics, Politicizing Law." *Law Contemporary Problems* 61: 41–68.

Frank, B. 1991. *The Decline of the Rule of Law in Singapore and Malaysia*. New York: The Association of the Bar of the City of New York.

Friedman, B. 2001. "The Counter-Majoritarian and the Pathology of Constitutional Scholarship." *Northwestern University Law Review* 95: 933–954.

Gibler, D. M., and K. A. Randazzo. 2011. "Testing the Effects of Independent Judiciaries on the Likelihood of Democratic Backsliding." *American Journal of Political Science* 55 (3): 696–709.

Ginsburg, T. 2003. *Judicial Review in New Democracies. Constitutional Courts in Asian Cases*. Cambridge: Cambridge University Press.

Ginsburg, T. 2010. "The Constitutional Court and the Judicialization of Korean Politics." In *New Courts in Asia*, edited by A. Harding and P. Nicholson, 145–157. London: Routledge.

Ginsburg, T. and A. Chen, eds. 2009. *Administrative Law and Governance in Asia. Comparative Perspectives*. London: Routledge.

Ginsburg, T., and T. Moustafa. 2008. *Rule by Law: The Politics of Courts in Authoritarian Regimes*. Cambridge: Cambridge University Press.

Ginsburg, T. and T. Matsudaira. 2012. "The Judicialization of Japanese Politics?" In *The Judicialization of Politics in Asia*, ed. B. Dressel, 17–37. Abingdon; New York: Routledge.

Goldstein, L. 2001. *Constituting Federal Sovereignty: The European Union in Comparative Context*. Baltimore: Johns Hopkins University Press.

Golub, S. 2003. "Beyond Rule of Law Orthodoxy: The Legal Empowerment Alternative" In *Rule of Law Series, Democracy and Rule of Law Project*. Washington: Carnegie Endowment for International Peace.

Graber, M. A. 2008. "The Countermajoritarian Difficulty: From Courts to Congress to Constitutional Order." *Annual Review of Law and Social Science* 4: 361–384.

Guarnieri, C. and P. Pederzoli, eds. 2002. *The Power of Judges*. New York: Oxford University Press.

Haley, J. 2006. *The Spirit of Japanese Law*. Athens: University of Georgia Press.

Haley, J. 2007. "Maintaining Integrity, Autonomy, and the Public Trust." In *Law in Japan: A Turning Point*, edited by D. Foote, 99–135. Seattle: University of Washington Press.

Harding, A. 2010. "The Constitutional Court of Thailand 1998–2006. A Turbulent Innovation." In *New Courts in Asia*, edited by A. Harding and P. Nicholson, 122–144. London: Routledge.

Harding, A., and P. Leyland. 2011. *The Constitutional System of Thailand. A Contextual Analysis*. Oxford: Hart Publishing.

Hewison, K. 2010. "Thailand's Conservative Democratization." In *East Asia's New Democracies. Deepening, Reversal, Non-Liberal Alternatives*, edited by Y.-W. Chu and S.-L. Wong, 122–140. London: Routledge.

Hilbink, L. 2008. "Assessing the New Constitutionalism." *Comparative Politics* 40 (2): 227–245.

Hirschl, R. 2004. *Towards Juristocracy: The Origins and Consequences of the New Constitutionalism.* Boston: Harvard University Press.

Hirschl, R. 2006. "The New Constitutionalism and the Judicialization of Pure Politics Worldwide." *Fordham Law Review* 75: 721–754.

Hirschl, R. 2008a. "The Judicialization of Mega-Politics and the Rise of Political Courts." *Annual Review of Political Science* 11: 93–118.

Hirschl, R. 2008b. "The Judicialization of Politics." In *The Oxford Handbook of Law and Politics*, edited by K. Whittington, D. Kelemen and G. Caldeira, 119–141. Oxford: Oxford University Press.

International Bar Association. 2008. *Prosperity versus Individual Rights? Human Rights, Democracy and Rule of Law in Singapore,* London.

Kaufmann, R., and A. Kraay. 2008. "Governance Indicators: Where Are We, Where Should We Be Going?" *World Bank Research Observer* 23 (1): 1–30.

Keong, C.S. 2010. "Judicial Review – From Angst to Empathy." *Singapore Academy of Law Journal* 22: 469–89.

Kim, J. 2010. "The Structure and Basic Principles of Constitutional Adjudication in the Republic of Korea." In *Litigation in Korea*, edited by K. Cho, 115–134. London: Edward Elgar.

Klein, J. 2003. "The Battle for the Rule of Law in Thailand: The Constitutional Court of Thailand." In *The Constitutional Court of Thailand. the Provisions and the Working of the Court*, edited by A. Raksasataya and J. Klein, 34–90. Bangkok: Constitution for the People Society.

Law, D. 2009. "The Anatomy of a Conservative Court: Judicial Review in Japan." *Texas Law Review* 87: 1545–1593.

Lee Kuan, Y. 2007. Speech to the International Bar Association Conference (October 14, 2007). http://app. subcourts.gov.sg/Data/Files/File/Speeches/2007Oct14_IBA_MMLeeKeynote.pdf.

Lee, Y. 2005. "Law, Politics, and Impeachment: The Impeachment of Roh Moo–Hyun from a Comparative Constitutional Perspective." *American Journal of Comparative Law* 53: 403–32.

Littlemore, S. 1998. "Report to the International Commission of Jurists Geneva, Switzerland, on a Defamation Trial in the High Court of Singapore, Goh Chok Tong vs J. B. Jeyaratnam. August 18–22," Unpublished report.

Matsui, S. 2011. "Why is the Japanese Supreme Court so Conservative?." *Washington University Law Review* 88: 1375–423.

McCargo, D. 2005. "Network Monarchy and Legitimacy Crisis in Thailand." *The Pacific Review* 18 (4): 499–518.

McCargo, D. 2008. "Thailand. State of Anxiety." In *Southeast Asian Affairs 2008,* edited by D. Singh and L. Salazar, 332–356. Singapore: Institute of South East Asian Studies.

Mietzner, M. 2010. "Political Conflict and Democratic Consolidation in Indonesia: The Role of the Constitutional Court." *Journal of East Asian Studies* 10 (3): 397–424.

Morton, F. 1995. "The Effect of the Charter of Rights on Canadian Federalism." *Publius* 25: 173–188.

Morton, F., and R. Knopff. 2000. *The Charter Revolution and the Court Party.* Peterborough: Broadview Press.

Nelson, M. 2006. "Political Turmoil in Thailand: Thaksin, Protests, Elections, and the King." *Eastasia. at* 5 (1): 1–22.

O'Brian, D., and Y. Ohkoshi. 2001. "Stifling Judicial Independence From Within: The Japanese Judiciary." In *Judicial Independence in the Age of Democracy: Critical Perspectives From Around the World*, edited by P. Russel and D. O'Brian, 37–61. Charlottesville: University of Virginia Press.

Park, J. 2008. "The Judicialization of Politics in Korea." *Asian-Pacific Law & Policy Journal* 10: 62–113.

Rajah, J. 2012. *Authoritarian Rule of Law: Legislation, Discourse and Legitimacy in Singapore*. Cambridge: Cambridge University Press.

Ramseyer, M. 1994. "The Puzzling (in)Dependence of Courts: A Comparative Approach." *Journal of Legal Studies* 23: 721–747.

Ramseyer, M. J., and E. B. Rasmusen. 2003. *Measuring Judicial Independence: The Political Economy of Judging in Japan*. Chicago: University of Chicago Press.

Rodan, G. 2004. *Transparency and Authoritarian Rule in Southeast Asia: Singapore and Malaysia*. London: Routledge.

Schmitt, C. 1958. *Verfassungsrechtliche Aufsätze aus den Jahren 1924–1954. Materialien zu einer Verfassungslehre*. Berlin: Duncker & Humblot.

Shankar, S. 2012. "The Judiciary, Policy, and Politics in India." *The Judicialization of Politics in Asia*, ed. B. Dressel, 56–77. Abingdon; New York: Routledge.

Shapiro, M., and A. Stone Sweet. 2002. *On Law, Politics, and Judicialization*. New York: Oxford University Press.

Sieder, R.L. Schjolden, and A. Angell eds. 2005. *The Judicialization of Politics in Latin America*. New York: Palgrave Macmillan.

Slaughter, A. 2000. "Judicial Globalization." *Virginia Journal of International Law* 40: 1103–1124.

Stone Sweet, A. 1999. "Judicialization and the Construction of Governance." *Comparative Political Studies* 32 (2): 147–184.

Stone Sweet, A. 2000. *Governing with Judges: Constitutional Politics in Europe*. Oxford: Oxford University Press.

Tate, N. 1994. "The Judicialization of Politics in the Philippines and Southeast Asia." *International Political Science Review* 15 (2): 187–197.

Tate, N. and T. Vallinder, eds. 1995. *The Global Expansion of Judicial Power*. New York: New York University Press.

Teubner, G. 1987. "Juridification – Concepts, Aspects, Limits, Solutions." In *Juridification of Social Spheres: A Comparative Analysis in the Areas of Labor, Corporate, Antitrust and Social Welfare Law*, edited by G. Teubner, 3–49. New York: de Gruyter.

Un, K. and S. So. 2012. "Cambodia's Judiciary: Heading for Political Judicialization?." In *The Judicialization of Politics in Asia*, ed. B. Dressel, 184–202. Abingdon; New York: Routledge.

Upham, F. 2005. "Political Lackeys or Faithful Public Servants? Two Views of the Japanese Judiciary." *Law & Social Inquiry* 30: 421–455.

Voigt, S., and E. Salzberger. 2002. "Choosing Not to Choose: When Politicians Choose to Delegate Powers." *Kyklos* 55: 289–310.

West, J., and D.-K. Yoon. 1992. "The Constitutional Court of the Republic of Korea: Transforming the Jurisprudence of the Vortex?" *American Journal of Comparative Law* 40: 73–119.

Worthington, R. 2001. "Between Hermes and Themis: An Empirical Study of the Contemporary Judiciary in Singapore." *Journal of Law and Society* 28 (4): 490–519.

Worthington, R. 2003. *Governance in Singapore*. London: RoutledgeCurzon.

Yeh, J.-R. 2010. "Presidential Politics and the Judicial Facilitation of Dialogue Between Political Actors in New Asian Democracies: Comparing the South Korean and Taiwanese Experiences." *International Journal of Constitutional Law* 8 (4): 911–949.

Yoon, D.-K. 2010. *Law and Democracy in South Korea – Democratic Development Since 1987*. Korea: Institute for Far Eastern Studies.

Pursuing Equity in Education: Conflicting Views and Shifting Strategies

LINDA CHELAN LI[*] & WEN WANG[**]

*Department of Public Policy, City University of Hong Kong, Hong Kong, China, **School of Public and Environmental Affairs, Indiana University-Purdue University Indianapolis, Indianapolis IN, USA

ABSTRACT   Under what circumstances will governments in developing countries, infamous for their "bad governance" records, adopt "good governance" institutions and practices, as defined and advocated by international development and donor organisations? What meanings are attached to these initiatives in the adopting countries and to what extent are they similar to those as understood in the developed countries? These questions are discussed in this article in the context of education equity reforms in China and America. Despite their divergent histories and economic and political systems, their experience in terms of education equity reforms is more similar than one would anticipate. Penetrating these similarities is the observation that understanding the specific historical contexts wherein "good governance" reforms have evolved is essential to a proper appreciation of the meanings and significance of the reforms, as institutions and mechanisms, for the furtherance of good governance as an outcome. The nuances of tension and heterogeneity of internal developments in each country, respectively, have interestingly also exposed the parallels between the processes in both.

Attaining equity in education provision is widely considered essential to providing each and every child with equal opportunities in life because it offers an adequate baseline to start their future development in the increasingly competitive globalised age. Education and equity have thus ranked prominently in development indices devised by international organisations.[1] A comparison of how equity in education has fared in the largest countries in the developing and developed worlds, respectively, should reveal valuable insights on the paths of good governance reforms in different contexts. This study examines the circumstances under which governments of developing countries adopt "good governance" institutions and practices, as defined and advocated by international development and donor institutions. It discusses the meanings attached to these initiatives in adopting countries and the extent to which they are similar to those as understood in developed countries. Specifically, it investigates the questions of whether education equity reforms in the US experience a different mix of difficulties and challenges as compared to reforms in

China, and whether the obviously different political systems and governance institutions in the two countries – one authoritarian and the other a democracy – mean that their education equity reforms would be impossible to compare.

By examining the trajectories of education equity policy in China and the US, we seek to highlight good governance policies in the context of their respective historical and social institutions, which have a direct impact for the meanings and implications of the policies. The meanings of education equity have been a subject of controversy and ongoing adjustments in both the US and China. Conflicting values of equity, efficiency, national coordination and local control have beset American society in addressing disparities in educational resources and outcomes across the country and slowed down improvements to reform design.

Previous reviews of school finance reforms in the US have acknowledged that it is not certain what *should* or *can* work to bring about education equity (National Research Council 1999). In China, education equity policies have emerged out of recurrent debates in society over the widening urban–rural divide as well as acute competition for places in "elite" schools. The modern concept of education equity, and what it means for government policy, is constantly "on the move" in both countries; the conceptual definition is still amorphous in China, given the shorter history of the policy discourse there. At the same time, largely reflective of the characteristics of the two political systems, the progress of reforms in the US was mediated through court litigation and decisions, whilst administrative actions have been the main driver of change in China. Nevertheless, despite their widely different histories and economic and political systems, reforms in the US and China share more similarities than one would expect. "Good governance" institutions are similarly a product in-the-making, notwithstanding the varied "good governance" records of the two countries. Discussion in this article thus drives home the message of historical institutionalism for change: that understanding the specific historical contexts wherein "good governance" reforms evolve is essential to a proper appreciation of the meanings and significance of the reforms, as institutions and mechanisms, for the furtherance of good governance as an outcome. Indeed, as the rest of the article shall show, it is through bringing out the nuances of tension and heterogeneity of internal developments in each society that the parallels between the processes in the two are also exposed.

United States: Equity or Adequacy?

Given the enormous resources involved in public education – nearly one-third of state and local spending in the US in 2009 (Barnett 2011) – and the critical private and societal benefits that it produces, few public policy areas have been more intensively studied, debated and acted upon in the US than the financing of primary and secondary education since the middle of the last century (See, for example, Moser and Rubenstein 2002; Beatty 2008). Indeed, debates about education can be traced to even earlier times and the development of a *public* education in today's largest developed democracy has not been free of political controversy (Ward 1998). At the time of the rise of the "common school movement" in the early–mid nineteenth century, there were views that schools should not be totally supported by the government without tuition fees. There was also an emerging position in favour of an equalisation of education opportunities through the provision of free schools to all. The different shades of opinions constituting each of three American ideational traditions – liberalism, republicanism and egalitarianism – mean that fundamental value conflicts have propelled and stalled changes of various sorts in society and public policy, including the development of public education (Rebell 1998).

Although the principle of universal free public education was established by the mid-nineteenth century as a result of the Common School Movement, which was part of a larger civic rights movement covering women's rights and anti-slavery at the time, there remained substantial differences within American society over what a "free" or "public" education was to constitute (Ward 1998; Burns 1982, 509–511). During colonial times, public schools were financed through a mix of local resources: taxation from properties, charity, revenues from public utilities, as well as tuition charges. Variations in local wealth thus meant variations in school funding and quality of public education across school districts. The strong emphasis on local control and citizens' choice in the liberal tradition has continued to reinforce local-based school funding long after universal public education becomes the norm. The egalitarianism tradition of "men are created equal" as engraved in the Declaration of Independence, on the other hand, has led some states to adopt language in state constitutions that makes support of education for all children a state responsibility. Quality public education for all requires higher taxes and often a redistribution of funds from wealthier districts to poorer ones. The conflict of egalitarian values with the conservatism in the Liberalism tradition, which is sometimes described as the "endowment effect" – entrenched local interests resisting all changes that may under-cut their privileges – has historically created a fertile ground for school funding disputes (Dayton and Dupre 2004; Ward 1998, 18).

Into the twentieth century and in particular since World War II, many changes have taken place. The Progressive Reform of the first half of the twentieth century saw reflection on the proper role of government in society. Equality of opportunity in educa-tion was much discussed and educationalists debated ways to define and achieve equality (Mort 1946; Morrison 1930; Ward 1998). The provision of public education was more accepted, along with a certain degree of equity in its provision (Ward 1998, 8–9). The implications for the regulatory power and redistributive functions of government repre-sented sharp breaks from past governmental policies and dispositions.

A landmark development indicating this egalitarianism tradition is the Federal Supreme Court's 1954 decision in *Brown v. Board of Education*, which declares unconstitutional state laws establishing separate public schools for black and white students (Dayton and Dupre 2004). Departing from previous emphasis on the value of decentralised control over educa-tion, it was ruled that "separate but equal" schools were inherently unequal (Moser and Rubenstein 2002). The country's awakening to the perils of unequal access to employment and education led to the enactment of a series of important federal laws. The Civil Rights Act of 1964, for example, mandated a study of the factors of unequal opportunity of education. The Coleman Report subsequently published in 1966 generated a long line of quantitative research, the findings of which stimulated further challenges to the status quo for equity reforms. While researchers still debate the role of money in educational achievement, school finance equity litigations have been heard in virtually every state, with school finance reforms directly mandated by court rulings or indirectly spurred by the threat of litigation.

Three Waves of School Finance Court Decisions

Three "waves" of court decisions have significantly influenced the development of equity standards for public education in the US in the last four decades. The first wave started with *Serrano v. Priest* in the California Supreme Court in 1971 and ended with the Supreme Court's decision in *San Antonio Independent School District v. Rodriguez* in 1973 (Heise 1995). In *Serrano*, reform advocates successfully argued that per-pupil funding should be substantially equal, and not dependent upon a local school district's property (Koski and Hahnel 2008). The victory was short-lived, however. The federal position on equal protection underlining *Serrano* was quashed by the Federal Supreme Court in 1973 in a narrow five-to-four decision in *Rodriguez*, which effectively closed the door to school finance challenges *via* federal courts (Koski and Hahnel 2008). It was ruled that education is not a "fundamental interest" under the Federal Constitution, so that the school finance system in the state (of Texas, and by implication in other states as well), unequal as it was, did not contravene the Federal Constitution, and that the state's interest in local control over education sufficed to justify the existing school funding system (Heise 1995).

The clash between competing egalitarian and liberal notions of educational opportunity is apparent in these litigations (Rebell 1998). Inequalities in educational funding deny children an equal starting point in the competitive race for individual advancement, thus impairing their opportunity to realise their full potential as individuals, which is a liberal value. Funding disparities also clash with the egalitarian value that calls for either equality of inputs (school expenditures) or outputs (student performance). However, the actions required to reduce funding disparities, say state redistribution of fiscal resources in favour of poorer school districts, or capping of school expenditures in well-resourced districts, all run against well-entrenched liberal values of local control. The conflict between aspects of liberal and egalitarian ideals has subsequently slowed the momentum for school finance reform, as equal opportunity of education lost its status as a fundamental interest in *Rodriguez* and a good proportion of state courts defended the status quo during the first wave of litigations (Ward 1998, 17).

The second wave of litigations, between 1973 and 1989, focused on forcing state legislatures and governments to reduce per-pupil spending disparities across school districts (Heise 1995), relying mainly on equal protection clauses in state constitutions. This wave of litigations yielded relatively few victories for plaintiffs (Lukemeyer 2003). Many courts upheld the existing school finance systems and adopted a classical liberal stance similar to the Supreme Court's analysis in *Rodriguez*, rejecting the egalitarian strand represented in the litigant's call for reform (Heise 1995). State courts ruling in favour of defendants of the status quo found a justification in local control of education, a value rooted in both the liberal and republican traditions, and maintained that there was no evidence of a failure of state responsibility to provide an *adequate* education for all, despite the varying levels of school funding across school districts (Rebell 1998). The uneven outcomes in the courts exposed a failure of equity theory in distinguishing school expenditures from other important variables that also affect educational opportunity, such as quality of school buildings, textbooks and curricula. This has subsequently led to an alternative theory rooted in the notion of adequacy in the third wave of school finance court decisions (Heise 1995).

The third wave, which began when the state supreme courts of Montana, Texas and Kentucky overturned the wealth-based school finance systems in 1989, focuses on the adequacy, or sufficiency, of education, rather than on equity defined as per-pupil spending disparities. An adequacy claim does not seek equalisation in funding among school districts, but seeks increased funding necessary to provide students with "adequate" educational opportunities and outcomes (Minorini and Sugarman 1999). A departure of the adequacy litigations from previous court cases is thus the absence of a demand for access to *equal* resources for all school districts (Ryan and Heise 2002). Under adequacy, a large part of existing funding inequalities across districts will still remain since districts that can fund a more-than-adequate education will be free to do so.

The shift from equity to adequacy might be traced to strategic considerations by school finance reform advocates when conducting the litigations (Koshi and Hahnel 2008). First, by relying on the education clauses of state constitutions, judges may be less concerned about creating undesirable spillovers in other areas of public policy.[2] Second, adequacy arguments flow naturally from the language of education clauses, which requires the legislature to provide a "thorough and efficient," "uniform," or "high quality" education to students. Third, an adequacy standard creates less conflict with the value of local control. The authority of wealthy districts to make decisions of educational spending need not be constrained because of a court order that requires resources to be provided to poor school districts under adequacy. Finally, an adequacy standard may be more appealing intuitively than other fairness standards. One may feel an injustice when some school children are not receiving a minimally adequate education, but may not feel the same way if one child receives a better education than another, as long as the former has an "adequate" education.

More fundamentally, politics matters, as Wong (1999) demonstrates in a study on school funding decisions. Specifically, geopolitical developments internationally in the 1980s might have had an impact on the shift to adequacy. Economic downturn and acute global competition (the "Japan as Number One" discourse) during the 1980s led to a growing awareness of the competitive shortcomings of schools.[3] A heightened sense of crisis thus emerged to see all American children receive an *adequate* basic education in order to participate effectively in the globalised competition. Empirical studies on the role of politics in state-level policymaking and in school finance equity have also demonstrated the positive relation, in quite significant measure, between the political inclination of the electorate and state policies (Wright et al. 1987). In particular, Wood and Theobald (2003) find that where the score of "citizen liberalism" in a state is high, state policies on school funding tend to be more liberal and in favour of enhancing equity. The more liberal states are also more likely to act upon court decisions in favour of funding equity. The shifts in political orientations and geopolitical contexts of the time explain why many state courts turned to the adequacy standard in the 1990s and ruled in favour of reform, in spite of previous positions defending the status quo (Rebell 1998).

Defining Education Equity Standards

How are the value conflicts and politics underlining reform, as described above, affecting the configurations of reform and the shifting definitions of equity standards in particular? Several questions can be identified in this regard (Berne and Stiefel 1984; Monk 1990). First, what should be equalised – spending per pupil, real resources per pupil, or students' test scores (Johnston and Duncombe 1998; Yinger 2004)? Most school finance reforms and court litigations have focused on spending per pupil as the object of equalisation (Johnston and Duncombe 1998). However, this measure is widely regarded as unsatisfactory, because it does not account for the fact that educational costs vary across school districts for reasons outside the control of school officials. To move from spending per pupil to real resources per pupil and student performance requires accounting for the cost differences that arise either from input prices, for example, teachers' salaries, or from factors that affect the learning environment and capacity of students, such as family background and student characteristics, which will require much more sophisticated policy instruments (Duncombe et al. 1996).

Besides the object of equalisation, we need a standard for evaluating the progress in achieving equity goals. Educational equity can be defined in terms of achievement of some *relative standard* where disparities in resources or outcomes among school districts are kept within a specific range. The extreme version of this standard is absolute equality between districts: education is uniform in all school districts. Wealth neutrality is another possible standard for relative equity, which is achieved when district wealth and district educational spending are not systematically correlated (Johnston and Duncombe 1998; Yinger 2004).

An *absolute standard* of equity is educational adequacy, which is achieved when students in every district receive an education that meets some minimum standard (Yinger 2004). To some, the focus on adequacy offers a promise of tackling problems that previous equity (equalisation)-oriented reforms have failed to remedy. Others consider adequacy as a discouraging retreat in the battle for basic fairness by perpetuating an education system that tolerates large disparities in available educational resources across territorial units and communities. To almost everybody, the concept of adequacy is an evolving one; there is no consensus on its meaning and the policy community has had only limited understanding about how and what would be required to achieve it (National Research Council 1999). There is no agreed-upon list of goals for an adequate education or a standard for the skills, competencies and knowledge necessary to serve those goals. Even if the legislature and courts were to craft those standards, the scientific base on which resources are matched to desired educational outcomes, given varying student characteristics, is not yet firmly established (Koski and Hahnel 2008).

Despite the absence of consensus and the limits to knowledge, people tend to agree that adequacy focuses on outputs and outcomes, whilst previous debates over education equity have focused on funding disparities, as a measurement of input, among school districts, with funding equalisation or wealth-neutral funding pursued as remedies. However, for definitional as well as practical purposes, the concept of adequacy seems less about the input-output distinction and more about its greater emphasis on absolute rather than relative standards. Adequacy demands the delineation of a minimum standard of education to be applicable to all districts, which may be about input, output as well as outcome. As long as people can agree on a view of the minimum level in the selected standard, the adequacy requirement appears to be more amenable to operationalisation and thus more achievable practically than the equalisation standard.

This last point becomes obvious when we consider the implication of the standards for local control. An absolute standard defines a minimum level for district resources or a minimum local tax effort, but does not restrict district spending above that level. A wealth neutrality standard can be consistent with variations in local preferences for education provided that they are not systematically correlated with district wealth. The standard that implies the most significant restriction on local preferences is the relative equity standard, to the extent that it requires the capping of the maximum resources that can be provided by districts for local education, as it clashes with longstanding values over free choice and local control (Johnston and Duncombe 1998).

State Strategies and Their Effectiveness

Nearly all of the 50 states have implemented some sort of school finance reforms since 1971. Most states have used a lump-sum per-pupil grant, referred to as foundation aid, to denote a minimum expenditure level, on top of which local revenue supplements may be added (Fisher 2007). To design a foundation aid programme, a state will select a foundation level which corresponds, more or less, to the decision on the standard of education the state will regard as adequate. Since a higher foundation level implies a higher cost of funding, each state has to balance the educational benefits of having a higher standard against its cost.

An alternative instrument is a power-equalising or guaranteed tax base (GTB) programme, which is basically a matching grant with a higher matching rate for lower-wealth districts to provide an equal per-pupil property tax base to each district (Yinger 2004). The key issue in a GTB plan is to determine the specific level of the guaranteed per-pupil tax base. If a state sets a guaranteed tax base close to the per-pupil property value in the wealthiest district, then every district in the state except the wealthiest receives some state assistance. A low guaranteed tax base, on the other hand, lowers the amount of state aid and the cost to the state. A provision of "recapture" may also be included in the GTB formula to restrict spending by wealthy districts through a negative matching rate and hence a higher local price of education (Yinger 2004).

The selection of a state aid mechanism is often guided by court decisions. Since many of the earlier state court decisions focused on disparity in education spending, GTB formulae tended to be more popular. The third wave of school finance court decisions, emphasising adequacy of education, has seen the foundation plan become the most popular state aid programme, which has since been adopted in the majority of the states (Yinger 2004).

Both the foundation and power-equalising grants have boosted total local spending on education, but not by the full amount of the grants, as a substantial amount of grant dollars are often used for local tax relief. Moreover, to the extent that the measures help with enhancing education equity, neither traditional foundation aids nor power-equalising programmes are fully effective in equalising per-pupil spending among districts, due to inelasticity of demand for education spending (Fisher and Leslie 2000). Partly to improve the efficacy of the instruments, since the 1990s there has been a search for alternative options, including more restrictive foundation programmes that include some form of mandatory minimum local fiscal effort and capping of spending or taxes for high-spending districts.

Setting a minimum tax rate for districts ensures a "foundational" amount of local fiscal contribution to education equivalent to the mandatory minimum tax rate. This measure should set off, to an extent, the replacement effect of state aid for local inputs in education; otherwise, districts receiving a relatively high amount of state aid might lower their tax rates to free up taxpayers' resources for other purposes. The decision concerning capping local supplementation in high-spending, usually wealthier, districts is more controversial, as it directly challenges the tradition of local control and, implicitly, the interests of the more privileged, as noted above. In both cases the tension between equity and centralisation on the one hand, and local choice, efficiency and decentralisation on the other, is evident, both in terms of public finance theory and practical politics, as people's opinions and interests vary and shift (Johnston and Duncombe 1998; Oates 2005,

2008). These tensions will be mitigated if adequacy is the desired equity standard, which focuses on the sufficiency of education provided to the least-funded locality or student against some perceived standards and objectives, rather than on relativity of performance (inputs and outputs) between localities or students. This perhaps also explains why adequacy has emerged as the preferred approach to define equity more recently.

Whatever the nuances in definition and standards, are the reforms of the past few decades effective in reducing inequities in school education? Assessments vary considerably and the prudent conclusion is that the results are mixed. On the one hand, there are those who suggest that reforms have *generally* achieved their goal of moving towards a more equitable distribution of resources (Evans et al. 1999; Reed 2001). One assessment states that, for example, the court-mandated reforms reduced within-state inequality by 19–34% between 1971 and 1996, depending on the measure of inequality employed (Evans et al. 1999). The reforms have also been found to be effective in increasing spending in low-wealth districts, though they are less successful in reducing spending in high-wealth districts (National Research Council 1999). The key issue for policymakers and courts is not whether the state should use education aid to equalise education spending, some have said, but how and by how much (Yinger 2004). More recently, the emphasis over adequacy of education has raised the question of whether state aid reform indeed improves student performance, rather than just equalising education spending (if at all). But given our current state of knowledge on input-outcome relations, this has proven to be a tricky issue (Ward 1998: 19).[4]

Others are sceptical of what the reform can deliver. In a review of the effects of litigation over school finance, Dayton (1996, 27) concludes that "judicial action can be *a useful tool* in the struggle for legislative attention and in the attempt to communicate to the electorate the need for equitable and adequate educational opportunities for all children" (emphasis added).

The emphasis is on the role of the litigations as part of the political processes of policy change. There are many actors in these processes, amongst whom are the courts and the litigants. The main effect of the litigations is *not* the degree of reduction of inequity in the school resources the litigations directly influence, even though the latter is the subject of the litigations. Rather, the litigations' effects are seen in how they shaped the ideas and behaviour of other actors, including the legislature, administrators and the electorate in the matter of school finance and education equity. This interpretation of the role of *any* piece of reform being realised through its *interaction* with related processes and other actors in the change process, cautioning against a mechanical measurement of direct effects and indeed a unilinear notion of causality, echoes an analysis made in 1930 by educationist Henry Morrison. When reviewing the effects of the early attempts of his time on state equalisation subvention, Morrison observed:

> The essential purpose of subvention…is *not* equalization, neither equalization of opportunity nor fiscal equalization. It is rather *the encouragement of local districts to undertake what they would not otherwise undertake* for the achievement of some purpose in public education which the state government thinks ought to be achieved (Morrison cited in Ward 1998, 11, emphasis added).

The education equity reform is, ultimately, a restructuring of the institutions and incentives to instil an appropriate set of ideas and dispositions for the desired behaviour. The assessment of any components and aspects of the reform process, be they the litigations or specific measures and policy instruments, has to be conducted and interpreted in this light.

China: Standards-In-The-Making

In socialist China as in the democratic US, basic education (primary and middle school) has long depended on local funding. This is especially the case after the decentralisation of state responsibilities in the 1980s, when the post-Mao leadership embarked upon the dismantling of the command economy framework. With limited investment from higher levels of the government, uneven economic development and varied fiscal capacities in different parts of the country, previous disparities in education spending across localities further widened (Wang and Zhao 2012). The turn to the market for additional resources to compensate for the shortfall of state investment did not help, as often better-endowed localities attracted the most additional investment. Access to education became a function of one's ability to pay. By the 1990s, complaints were commonplace over pricy "elite" schools beyond the means of the average urban residents, and over rundown rural schools whose upkeep both parents and local governments could not afford (Tsang 2000).

Early Discussions

In comparison to the US, the emergence in China of a policy discourse on education equity is a more recent phenomenon: in 2004 the term "education equity" (*jiaoyu junheng*) appeared for the first time in the text of a central government document (Ministry of Education of PRC et al. 2004). Nevertheless, despite the lack of an explicit mention, the notion of equity, or more precisely inequity, had been central to heated debates over education in society. At least 20 central government documents were issued between 1991 and 2010, for example, to demand tighter control over the fees charged by elite schools to prospective students. The "switching school" phenomenon, whereby parents voted with their feet against the laxly enforced "school where you live" policy to pursue better educational opportunities for their children, has further accentuated the imbalance of distribution over educational resources across schools. As the quality of education in weaker and less well-endowed schools dropped further due to loss of senior teachers to elite schools, the exodus of teachers continued and deepened the vicious cycle. At the same time, the fees to secure a place in a top-ranked school shot up, generating grievances both amongst those who were priced out of the schools and those getting in.

Rural education is another major site of grievances over inequities. Fiscal centralisation in the mid-1990s had raised more revenues for the central coffers at the expense of local revenues, while local governments were loaded with a lengthening list of responsibilities from agriculture to industrial development, medical insurance, pensions, education, culture and social control. This resulted in the infamous "unfunded mandate" syndrome as commensurable amounts of government funds were not made available to finance the responsibilities (Wong 1997; World Bank 2002). To meet these ends, local governments and schools turned to parents to pay teachers and even school electricity bills. The rural tax reform in the early 2000s banned many excessive fees (Li 2012). The result, however, was that many rural schools suffered a fiscal crisis as no alternative funding had been provided. Many schools shut down, not being able to pay even minimal costs (Li and Wu 2005; Wang and Zhao 2012). Whilst education inequity in cities was about differences between a privileged few schools and the majority, in many parts of rural China the question was whether classes could continue and students actually get *some* education.

Yet another issue of education inequity that caught public and media attention was the education of the children of migrant workers (Xiang 2005). These children were caught in a no-win situation. Accompanying their parents in their new urban homes, many struggled to find a place in urban public schools, which they were often denied access to due to their official rural household status. Most of these children ended up studying in social schools operated by local groups with a meagre budget and, obviously, substandard facilities. Those children not travelling with their migrant parents and staying in their rural homes faced another sort of nightmare – potential neglect, which along with a whole range of developmental and sociological problems have been identified as, summarily, the "Left Behind Children Syndrome" (Wu and Yang 2005; Zhou et al. 2005).

An Evolving Concept and Agenda

These discussions over problems in urban and rural education gradually crystallised into an explicit policy of education equity. An online search of the literature in the China Journals Full-text Database (CJFD) using "the equitable development of compulsory education" (*yiwu jiaoyu junheng fazhan*) as title keywords gives a total of 743 articles between 1994 and 22 October 2010, with 36 articles during the decade of 1994–2004, and 707 articles in the five years since 2005. Most articles in the earlier period discuss funding deficits. There was no attempt to define education equity or to delineate measures to improve equity. The watershed moment came in 2004–05. In 2004, enhancing education equity was explicitly prescribed in a Ministry of Education document on combating illegal fees in the educational sector as an "important measure" to deal with the "switching schools" issue. Local governments were urged to "take up the responsibility for improving equity, devise effective measures to make available more education resources, and elevate the standards and quality of education in the weaker schools" (Ministry of Education of PRC 2004). The Ministry of Education (2005) issued *Some Opinions on Further Enhancing the Equitable Development of Compulsory Education*, which is the first document issued by a central ministry with "equitable development of education" (*jiaoyu junheng fazhan*) prominently in its title. The 2005 document marks the beginning of a new chapter in education policy: as a universal basic-level of education has been attained, 20 years after the promulgation of the goal in the 1986 Education Law, it is time to move on.

The 2005 document lays out an approach for implementing the new objective of education equity. The major grievance over inequities has been the differential access to educational resources in schools in different territorial units. A first step is thus to specify a territorial scope wherein such differences should be narrowed. This territorial scope is defined as the county/district level. In other words, equity improvement efforts will seek to reduce the gaps in education between towns and townships, the constituent urban and rural territorial units within a county. There is still, however, no specific definition of "education equity" in the document, though there is an elaborate discussion of the need to reduce the increasing disparities in educational resources. Measures listed include more funding to weaker schools and localities, stricter control over school switching, and improving teachers' training and resources (such as teacher–student ratio and school facilities). Provincial governments were also urged to enhance their role, though what it means practically speaking is not at all clear.

The new policy emphasis on education equity quickly led to a blossoming of studies on the subject. As noted above, the 707 articles with "education equity" in their titles in the five years from 2005 are almost 20-fold the number of studies recorded in the CJFD during the previous decade (Du and Sun 2009). Mirroring the societal discussion and policy emphasis, scholarly studies show a similar concentration on a relative standard of equity, and stress the importance of narrowing, gradually, the disparity in educational resources across various definitions of jurisdictions and boundaries. However, similar to the official documents, no clear definition of the concept of equity is offered. While discussion focuses on the need to reduce disparities, there is no delineation of *how large* a disparity at any time will be unacceptable for the criterion of equity.

In January 2010, the Ministry of Education issued *An Opinion to Further Enhance the Equitable Development of Compulsory Education as a Measure to Implement the Scientific Development Strategy*, which further develops the education equity policy in a number of ways. First, it outlines a phased approach, setting the year 2012 for achieving "preliminary" equity in education, and 2020 for "basic" equity. Again, there is no explicit definition of what counts as "preliminary" (*chubu*) and "basic" (*jiben*) equity, but a "gradual" progression in the reduction of disparity has apparently been taken to differentiate the two phases.[5] A second development is a designation of the respective roles of different levels of government over the reduction of inequities. The provincial level will provide coordination and guidance, and formulate the basic education standards for implementation at schools. It will also design measures to support weaker localities within the provincial boundary. The prefectural (city) level is charged with the formulation of detailed plans of action, which the county will execute.

Two points are worth noting. The first is the delineation of roles of government at various levels. This reflects an understanding that reducing inequities in schools requires a larger role for the upper tiers of government as often the redistribution of resources across jurisdictions of varying means is necessary. Second, there is for the first time an explicit mention of the need to formulate school-based education standards, in addition to the traditional emphasis on meeting funding needs. The new emphasis on common standards begs questions of *what* the standards are and *how* they are determined. More importantly, setting common standards to be applicable to all suggests a shift to an absolute standard of equity – a *minimum* level of "adequate" education, as opposed to a relative standard emphasising equalisation or reduction of differences in the quality and resources of education.

Probing for a Strategy

Whilst court decisions have had a conspicuous presence in education equity reform in the US, in China the locus of events was mostly within the administration, though the increasingly active virtual space of the netizen community is posing an increasing influence on policy (see Lewis 2013). "Informal" sources, such as officials' elaboration of policy in media interviews, speeches and articles, offer important insights into aspects of the policymaking process, supplementing the formal sources of policy documents and regulations.

In a national education conference in late 2009, a few weeks before the production of the 2010 document, the deputy director of the Compulsory Education Bureau of the Ministry of Education briefed conference participants regarding the ongoing debates for and against the promulgation of a common national standard for the quality of education (Yang 2009). Supporters of a common national standard saw in it guaranteed access to education of a similar quality for all children. Opponents stressed the need for diversity in education, in view of the long-standing local characteristics in a continent-sized country, and doubted the feasibility and possible negative repercussions of a common standard. Whilst noting the controversy of the issue, Yang made clear his preference for the delineation of a common *minimal* standard, so that all children will be guaranteed at least a certain minimal standard of education, *in order to attain some degree of equity.* Yang (2009) stated: "This standard will provide a 'floor' for all, and it brings no capping of the upper end beyond it. At least we need a floor, or else how can we still claim we are to improve equity?" This reference to a "floor" was repeated by Gao Hong, Yang's senior at the Compulsory Education Bureau, in another media interview explaining the 2010 document.

> The overall strategy is…to take education equity reform as a means towards a better quality of education…we make it clear that equitable development (of education) does not imply capping the strong in order to elevate the weak. *Rather it is to gradually elevate the standards of education across the board as we advance on the front of equity* (Gao 2010, emphasis added).

The reference to a "floor" in the Chinese context is similar to the foundation grants of states and the adequacy concept of equity in the US, upheld by many state courts as the preferred standard of equity since the 1980s: since all students had access to a minimum, basic education, the school finance system was not unconstitutional despite disparities in its educational quality and equality (Verstegen 1998). Given the acute concerns over relative inequity in education in Chinese society since the 1990s, the arrival of an absolute minimal standard and the explicit denial of plans to cap the upper end of the continuum remind us of the criticism of retreat in the US over adequacy.

There is also an explicit reference to a *dynamic* notion of equity in Gao's articulation of the minimum standard, with the "floor" moving upwards to a higher standard over time. A similar note was also heard in US courts in the 1990s. When discussing how to define standards of education adequacy in a changing society, it was maintained that "what was adequate in the past is inadequate today" (Verstegen 1998). The floor will be shifting upwards in an escalating "spiral" over time. A theoretical possibility is that the successive elevation of the "floor," if sustained long enough, will lead to an eventual closing of the gaps between strong and weaker schools. Or the floor can become so sufficiently high that other schools "above" the floor will not materially cause any substantive injustice or deprivation.

Underlying the strategy of a minimum standard of education is the broader policy of "equalisation of basic public services." Emerging out of two discourses on the role of government and widening regional disparities, respectively, in the 1990s, the notion of "equalisation of basic public services" reflects an attempt to delineate the boundary of the government's role and responsibility to ensure an adequate provision of public services across the variably endowed regions in the country. The overriding concern is the growing disparity in the level of service provision, and in particular the low level of provision in some areas. "Equalisation" has been officially described, in that regard, as a "necessary strategy towards achieving co-ordinated development of different regions and narrowing regional disparities" (Hu 2007), but its precise meaning has been rather ambivalent, from an initial emphasis on "equalising" – reducing and eliminating differences – to the more recent interpretation of having a "basic," or minimum, standard of provision for all (Liu 2010).

So far the most important policy instrument at work to serve the policy objective of improving education equity has been the Fund Guarantee Mechanism (FGM). In the early 2000s, the central government implemented the Rural Tax Reform to contain the excessive extraction of revenue in the countryside in light of rising threats to social stability and regime legitimacy. To compensate for the loss of revenues historically supporting rural education, in 2006 the FGM was instituted to provide rural schools in the more deprived regions of the country with a "floor" of funding, largely from central and provincial coffers (State Council 2005). Through enacting common standards for provision, and gradually elevating the standard of provision, the FGM provides a mechanism to increase the resources available to weaker schools and localities and thus raise education quality gradually. Equity in education will be improved through "lifting" the "floor" from the bottom end. From 2006 to 2011, nearly 500 billion *yuan* of additional funding from central and provincial coffers has been injected into rural schools, mostly in the economically weak central and western regions. The levels of subsidies to school operation costs, on a per student basis, have been raised four times, from RMB 150/250 (primary/middle school) in 2007, to 300/500 in 2009, 400/600 in 2010, and up to 500/700 in 2011.

Apart from the lifting of the "funding floor," another initiative was to formulate an education equity index, which in 2009 involved 312 counties participating in a national "pilot" scheme and several pioneering provincial governments (Ministry of Education of PRC 2009; Chongqing City Government 2010). One objective of the pilot scheme was to gain experience in gathering *precise* and *detailed* information on the existing situation of education provision, including the extent of disparities, which is essential for the development of education standards and classification of the "floor" (Chen 2009). In fact, the lack of good data has not only impaired the assessment of education equity but also its implementation by local governments. The heavy reliance on funds from higher levels of government has also brought issues of agency control and efficiency. Somewhat similar to the effect of state grants on local tax relief in the US, the additional FGM funding from the central-provincial governments has had a "crowding out" effect on local educational spending, as local governments diverted local resources to other policy areas (Li and Yuan 2011). By 2012, a full system of national education standards had been put in place to monitor the progress of education equity in the counties and provinces. For the first time, the central government clearly delineates the required education equity standard based on a composite measure of resources for schools within a county (Ministry of Education of PRC 2012).

In comparison to various distinctive education aid designs adopted by individual states in the US, China has mainly pushed for more educational funding from the central and provincial governments for localities all over the country. The major policy objective has been to define and guarantee the minimum "floor" of funding for education.

Conclusions

Both China and the US have pressed the need for a good education at the turn of the twenty-first century. In 1994, the US Congress enacted the Goals 2000: Educate America Act mandating provisions to ensure "students can learn and achieve to high standards," noting that students "must realise their potential if the United States is to prosper." In 2002, President Bush signed the No Child Left Behind Act into law, which was designed to improve student achievement and to hold states and schools more accountable to student progress. Also in 1994, the Chinese government stepped up the implementation of compulsory basic-level education for all children in the 6–15 age cohorts, pledged in the 1986 Education Law, leading to ambitious school building programmes across the country (Ministry of Education 1994). In 2005, a decade after the Educate America Act was enacted, education equity was formally placed on the national policy agenda in China. New central funds of an unprecedented scale were provided to the financially weak regions to enhance education quality in schools. In both the US and China, policy discussions on education equity were embedded in concerns in society over the quality of education students received, as well as over broader issues and values of local autonomy, fairness, social stability and regime legitimacy. In both countries actions for change started with adjustments to government funding. Policy strategies were devised to reduce the funding gaps and, similarly, there has been a gradual shift in emphasis from equalisation of education funding towards a minimum standard of adequacy, which in turn leads to the definition of educational standards.

These common trends between the two countries have co-existed with important differences, which serve not to offset the similarities but inform them, to enable a deeper appreciation of the trends and anticipation of possible future developments. Table 1 shows a comparison of education finance reforms in the US and China. One difference lies in the movement from equity to adequacy in each country. Despite the apparent parallels, in China there has not been an explicit articulation of the shift as in the US, where numerous studies have debated the concept of adequacy *vis-à-vis* equity. Indeed an equivalent term for "adequacy" has yet to emerge in the Chinese discourse, where the most used terms are "equity" (*junheng*), "equalisation" (*jundenghua*), "fairness" (*gongping*) and "equality" (*pingdeng*) (Liu 2010). The notions of a "floor" or "baseline" (*dixian*) that have appeared in academic studies and the speeches of education officials should be closest to

Table 1. Education equity reforms in the United States and China

	United States	China
Changes in education equity standards	Shifted from equity (a relative standard) to adequacy (an absolute standard)	No explicit shift in standards; the concept of adequacy has yet to emerge
Strategies to achieve education equity	Guaranteed tax base (GTB) and foundation programmes	A larger spending commitment by the central and provincial governments, e.g., Fund Guarantee Mechanism (FGM)
Drivers of education finance reforms	Value conflicts in American society; the three waves of court decisions; state government actions	Concerns over disparities in educational resources and outcomes in the communities and policy circles; party–state administration

"adequacy" in the US context, but they were used in China to explain what "equalisation" or "equity," which appear in the official texts, actually mean in terms of practical consequence. In other words, the deed is still in search of the right name, and the semantic confusion sometimes has led to conceptual ambiguities. The adequacy discourse in the US has, on the other hand, gone beyond the prescription of a basic or minimum standard of educational programme that was deemed acceptable three decades ago (Verstegen 1998), to a more precise definition of *what in the contents of the education process and outcomes define an "adequate" or "sufficient" education.* Central to this is the curriculum. There is also an increasing awareness that our knowledge on this question – the linkage between input and expected outcome – is limited (National Research Council 1999). It is, for example, difficult to predict or anticipate what children will *need* to know or be equipped with for their future, given the rapidly changing society. Efforts to pin down some sort of an answer to this question have led to the emerging movement of education standards, including an ongoing debate on whether federal common standards should be developed for voluntary adoption (Beatty 2008).[6] The idea of national standards seems easier to come by in China, which has recently put in place a national evaluation framework, despite a late start to the conceptual discussion. Here the more centralised political tradition of China is likely to be instrumental.

With regard to strategies, both countries have adopted centralisation of some sorts in their equity reforms. In response to the early court decisions, several states in the US implemented GTB programmes to meet the equalisation standard. With greater emphasis on adequacy in later years, the foundation plan has become the most popular aid programme. Common to either instrument is the state-level's intervention in local education finance. In China, the FGM is explicitly a scheme of intergovernmental transfers through earmarked funds to schools. The requirements for local matching funds and imposition of provincial and national standards also spell an enlarged role of the central and provincial governments in local education. Indeed, as fundamental value conflicts in American society have permeated reforms in the US, equity reforms in China have similarly accentuated traditional concerns over agency control and implementation efficiency.

Another point of interest is the process through which change was driven. Litigation resulting from fundamental value conflicts in society played a critical role in the US, having started the school finance reform movement in the early years, though state governments have also initiated reforms independent of court decisions. In China, given widespread concerns in society and academic circles over the unequal distribution of educational resources and outcomes, the party–state administration has remained the major venue in which critical decisions are made. In both countries inter-governmental relations have loomed large. In the US, the states have been critical players, demanding and supplementing actions of the local districts. Even the Federal Government has increasingly been drawn in, through executive orders and legislations, despite the earlier constitutional ruling against a definitive federal role. In China, the policy on education equity emerged as part of the central government's broader objective of improving local provision of basic public services, mostly through a larger spending commitment from the central and provincial coffers. On the one hand, a stepped-up role for the regional levels is necessary to correct imbalances in local resource allocation in education, the roles of state governments in the US and central government in China have nevertheless been criticised, as the negative impacts of the equity reforms for local control and efficiency have surfaced (Johnston and Duncombe 1998; Li and Yuan 2011). To the extent that the trade-off between equity and efficiency, and national direction and local control, reveals a conflict between fundamental values and is thus "irresolvable," how to strike a compromise between the simultaneous demands will inform, to a large measure, the future trajectory of education equity policy in the US and China. Finding a way in which the various levels of government may work together more effectively will be a common challenge for the two countries in their shared objective to deliver a good education for all American and Chinese children, as well as for future research.

Acknowledgements

The research for this article was generously supported by a General Research Grant awarded by the Hong Kong Research Grant Council, "Demarcating the Responsibilities of Government across Tiers in China: Reform Discourse, Change Processes, and Significance" (CityU 9041606). We are thankful for the quality research assistance of project assistants Drs Liu Ying and Roger Yang. An earlier version of this article was presented at the International Workshop on "Good Governance in the Asia-Pacific Region: Civil and Political Society," City University of Hong Kong, 9–10 December 2010. We are grateful for the comments from the participants. We are particularly thankful to Robert Gregory who was discussant to the article at the Workshop and the anonymous reviewers of this journal for their invaluable suggestions to further improve the article.

Notes

[1] Education features in, amongst others, the Human Development Index (United Nations Development Program) and Sustainable Governance Indicators (Seyfried 2011). Equity is explicitly listed amongst the three major values (with sustainable development and peace) in the World Governance Indicators (World Bank), is one of the four in the Urban Governance Index (United Nations Human Settlements Programme) (with accountability, participation and effectiveness), and one of the eight major characteristics constituting "good governance practices" (with accountability, transparency, responsiveness, effectiveness and efficiency, rule of law, participation and consensus), according to the Economic and Social Conditions Committee for Asia and the Pacific of the United States.

[2] Views on this matter are at best tentative, however. Lukemeyer (2003) finds that the hypothesis that courts defining their constitutions as imposing an adequacy standard were more likely to rule in favour of plaintiffs cannot be supported. While courts were more likely to accept an adequacy standard, they were also more likely to find the standard met.

[3] For an example, see the controversial *The Closing of the American Mind*, by Alan D. Bloom (1987).

[4] The relevance of school-related inputs and educational outcomes was once again questioned during the Chicago teachers' strike in September 2012. The strike triggered heated debates over the need for a broader approach beyond the education/school budget to the dire inequities in educational outcomes in Chicago schools and in the US generally (see Angert 2012).

[5] It is stated that "the focus for most localities will be to enhance equity in education within the boundary of a county-district, whilst others with the means will improve inter-county equity." When "basic equity" is achieved by 2020, "the educational resources and quality of education in rural schools will be further improved, and the mechanisms for education equity will be further perfected" (Ministry of Education 2010, paragraphs 2 and 4).

[6] By 2008, all 50 states had established their respective, and varied, standards for education from kindergarten through grade 12, including both content standards (which describe material that students are to learn) and performance standards (which describe the level of proficiency expected). The current debate is about options to improve state standards and how standards can best improve education results, including the development of voluntary federal standards.

References

Angert, B. 2012. "Unions, Education and The Chicago Teachers Strike," *OpEdNews*, September 23, Accessed December 20, 2013. http://www.opednews.com/articles/Unions-Education-and-The-by-Betsy-L-Angert-120923-207.html

Bank, W. 2002. *China: National Development and Sub-National Finance: A Review of Provincial Expenditures.* Washington DC: World Bank.

Barnett, J. 2011. "State and Local Governments Finances Summary: 2009." Washington D.C.: Governments Division Briefs, United States Census Bureau. Accessed August 1, 2012 http://www2.census.gov/govs/estimate/09_summary_report.pdf

Beatty, A. 2008. *Common Standards for K-12 Education? Considering the Evidence: Summary of a Workshop Series.* Washington DC: National Academic Press.

Berne, R., and L. Stiefel. 1984. *The Measurement of Equity in School Finance: Conceptual, Methodological and Empirical Dimensions.* Baltimore: Johns Hopkins University Press.

Bloom, A. 1987. *The Closing of the American Mind.* New York: Simon & Schuster.

Burns, J. 1982. *The Vineyard of Liberty.* New York: Vintage Books.

Chen, W. 2009. "*Guanyu yiwu jiaoyu junheng fazhan dudao pinggu tixi de sikao.*" (Thought on supervision and evaluation mechanism of compulsory education equity development). Accessed September 9, 2012. http://hxjy.com/v2templet/pg_interchange.asp?id=383&lm=%E5%AD%A6%E6%9C%AF%E9%A2%91%E9%81%93

Chongqing City Government. 2010. "*Chongqingshi yiwu jiaoyu junheng fazhan hege quxian dudao pinggu fangan.*" (Evaluation plan of compulsory education equalisation of Chongqing City) Accessed November 2, 2010. http://code.fabao365.com/law_506210_1.html.

Dayton, J. 1996. "Examining the Efficacy of Judicial Involvement in Public School Funding Reform." *Journal of Education Finance* 22 (1): 1–27.

Dayton, J., and A. Dupre. 2004. "School Funding Litigation: Who's Winning the War?." *Vanderbilt Law Review* 57 (6): 2351–2413.

Du, Y., and Z. Sun. 2009. Zhongguo yiwu jiaoyu caizheng yanjiu. Research on Compulsory Education Financing in China). Beijing: Beijing Normal University Press.

Duncombe, W., J. Ruggiero, and J. Yinger. 1996. "Alternative Approaches to Measuring the Cost of Education." In *Holding Schools Accountable: Performance-Based Reform in Education,* edited by H. Ladd, 327–356. Washington DC: The Brookings Institution.

Evans, W., S. Murray, and R. Schwab. 1999. "The Impact of Court-Mandated School Finance Reform." In *Equity and Adequacy in Education Finance: Issues and Perspectives,* edited by H. Ladd, R. Chalk, and J. Hansen, 72–98. Washington DC: National Academy Press.

Fisher, R. 2007. *State & Local Public Finance.* 3rd ed. Mason: Thomson Higher Education.

Fisher, R., and P. Leslie. 2000. "Local Government Responses to Education Grants." *National Tax Journal* 53 (1): 153–168.

Gao, H. 2010. "*Junhe fazhan shi yiwu jiaoyu zhongzhong zhizhong de renwu.*" (Equitable development is the most important task in compulsory education). Interview in Zhongguo Jiaoyu Bao (China Education Daily). Accessed October 28. http://jijiao.jyb.cn/jd/201001/t20100113_335200_1.html

Goals 2000: Educate America Act. 1994. P. L. 103–227, Section 30(1). Washington DC: The 103rd Congress of the United States.

Heise, M. 1995. "State Constitutions, School Finance Litigation, and the 'Third Wave': From Equity to Adequacy." *Temple Law Review* 68: 1151–1176.

Hu, J. 2007. *Report of the Central Committee of the Sixteenth Party Congress to the Seventeenth Party Congress Plenum.* Accessed September 6, 2010. http://news.sina.com.cn/c/2007-10-24/205814157282.shtml

Johnston, J., and W. Duncombe. 1998. "Balancing Conflicting Policy Objectives: The Case of School Finance Reform." *Public Administration Review* 58 (2): 145–158.

Koski, W., and J. Hahnel. 2008. "The Past, Present and Possible Futures of Educational Finance Reform Litigation." In *Handbook of Research in Education Finance and Policy,* edited by H. Ladd and E. Fiske, 42–60. New York: Routledge.

National Research Council. 1999. "Making Money Matter: Financing America's Schools." In *Committee on Education Finance, Commission on Behavioral and Social Sciences and Education,* edited by H. Ladd and J. Hansen, Washington DC: National Academy Press.

Lewis, O. 2013. "Net Inclusion: New Media's Impact on Deliberative Politics in China,." *Journal of Contemporary Asia* 43 (4): 678–708.

Li, L. 2012. *Rural Tax Reform in China: Policy Processes and Institutional Change.* London: Routledge.

Li, L., and L. Wu. 2005. "'Daobi' Haishi 'Fan Daobi': Nongcun Shuifei Gaige Qianhou Zhongyang Yu Defang Zhijian De Hudong" (Pressure for Changes: Central-Local Interactions in Rural Tax-for-Fee Reform)." *Shehuixue Yanjiu Sociological Research* 20 (4): 44–63.

Li, L., and F. Yuan. 2011. "Zhixin chaju yu shiquan huafen de panduan yuanze: jiaoyu gaige de zhichu fenxi" (Implementation gap and criteria on intergovernmental jurisdiction zoning: an analysis of school finance reform). *Zhongguo Nongcun Yanjiu* (Rural China Studies).

Liu, M. 2010. *"Woguo Jiben Gonggong Fuwu Lilun Yanjiu Pingshu"* (Theoretical Studies on "Basic Public Services": A Literature Review)." *Jingji Yanjiu Cankao (Review of Economic Research)* 16: 64–72.

Lukemeyer, A. 2003. *Courts as Policymakers: School Finance Reform Litigation.* New York: LFB Scholarly Publishing.

Ministry of Education of PRC. 1994. *A Temporary Regulation on Assessing and Monitoring the Implementation of Compulsory Basic Education.* Accessed November 15, 2010. http://202.205.177.9/edoas/website18/73/info6273.htm

Ministry of Education of PRC. 2004. *Guanyu 2004 nian zhili jiaoyu luanshoufei gongzuo de shishi yijian* (An opinion to implement the work on combating against the proliferation of illegal fees in education in 2004). Accessed November 3, 2010. http://jyb.cn.ht/edoas/website18/06/info18706.htm

Ministry of Education of PRC. 2005. *"Guanyu jinyibu tuanjin yiwu jiaoyu junhe fazhan de rogan yijian"* (Some opinions on further enhancing the equitable development of compulsory education). Accessed October 5, 2010. http://fagui.eol.cn/html/200909/1435_2.shtml

Ministry of Education of PRC. 2009. *Guanyu kaizhan yiwu jiaoyu junhe fazhan dudao pinggu shidian yanjiu gongzuo de tongzhi* (A notice on launching the pilot studies on assessing and monitoring education equity). Monitoring Bureau. Accessed November 2, 2010. http://www.gxedu.gov.cn/Item/262.aspx

Ministry of Education of PRC. 2010 *"Guanyu guance luoshi kexue fazhanguan jinyibu tuanjin yiwu jiaoyu junhe fazhan de yijian"* (An opinion to further enhance the equitable development of compulsory education). Accessed August 22, 2011. http://www.china.com.cn/policy/txt/2010-01/19/content_19269004.htm

Ministry of Education of PRC. 2012. "Jiaoyu bu guanyu yinfa 'xianyu yiwu jiaoyu junheng fazhan dudao pinggu zanxing banfa' de tongzhi" (A notice of the Ministry of Education on the issuance of 'the temporary measures for monitoring and evaluating the equitable development of compulsory education within a county'). Accessed July 10, 2012 http://www.moe.gov.cn/publicfiles/business/htmlfiles/moe/moe_1789/201205/136600.html

Minorini, P., and S. Sugarman. 1999. "School Finance Litigation in the Name of Educational Equity: Its Evolution, Impact, and Future." In *Equity and Adequacy in Education Finance: Issues and Perspectives*, edited by H. Ladd, R. Chalk and J. Hansen, 34–71. Washington DC: National Academy Press.

Monk, D. 1990. *Education Finance: An Economic Approach.* New York: McGraw Hill.

Morrison, H. 1930. *School Revenue.* Chicago: University of Chicago Press.

Mort, P. 1946. *Principles of School Administration.* New York: McGraw-Hill.

Moser, M., and R. Rubenstein. 2002. "The Equality of Public School District Funding in the United States: A National Status Report." *Public Administration Review* 62 (1): 63–72.

Oates, W. 2005. "Toward a Second-Generation Theory of Fiscal Federalism." *International Tax and Public Finance* 12: 349–373.

Oates, W. 2008. "On the Evolution of Fiscal Federalism: Theory and Institutions." *National Tax Journal* 61 (2): 313–334.

Rebell, M. 1998. "Fiscal Equity Litigation and the Democratic Imperative." *Journal of Education Finance* 24 (1): 23–50.

Reed, D. 2001. *On Equal Terms: The Constitutional Politics of Educational Opportunity.* Princeton: Princeton University Press.

Ryan, J., and M. Heise. 2002. "The Political Economy of School Choice." *Yale Law Journal* 111: 2043–2136.

Seyfried, M. 2011. "Management Index Findings for the SGI 2011: A Comparison of Performance in Governance among OECD States." In *Sustainable Governance Indicators 2011. Policy Performance and Governance Capacities in the OECD*, edited by Bertelsmann Stiftung. 119–144. No place: Verlag Bertelsmann Stiftung. Accessed September 24, 2012. http://www.sgi-network.org/index.php?page=download_2011

State Council of PRC. 2005. *A Notice on Deepening the Fund Guarantee Mechanism of Rural Compulsory Education.* Document 43. Beijing: State Council of PRC.

Tsang, M. 2000. "Education and National Development in China Since 1949: Oscillating Policies and Enduring Dilemmas." In *China Review*, edited by C. Lau and J. Shen, 579–618. Hong Kong: The Chinese University of Hong Kong.

Verstegen, D. 1998. "Judicial Analysis During the New Wave of School Finance Litigation: The New Adequacy in Education." *Journal of Education Finance* 24 (1): 51–68.

Wang, W., and Z. Zhao. 2012. "Rural Taxation Reforms and Compulsory Education Finance in China." *Journal of Public Budgeting, Accounting, and Financial Management* 24 (1): 136–162.

Ward, J. 1998. "Conflict and Consensus in the Historical Process: The Intellectual Foundations of the School Finance Reform Litigation Movement." *Journal of Education Finance* 24 (1): 1–22.

Wong, C. ed. 1997. *Financing Local Government in the People's Republic of China.* Hong Kong: Oxford University Press.

Wong, K. 1999. *Funding Public Schools.* Lawrence: University Press of Kansas.

Wood, B., and N. Theobald. 2003. "Political Responsiveness and Equity in Public Education Finance." *The Journal of Politics* 65 (3): 718–738.

Wright, G., R. Erikson, and J. McIver. 1987. "Popular Control of Public Policy in the American States." *American Journal of Political Science* 31 (4): 980–1001.

Wu, L., and Z. Yang. 2005. "*Guanai Kongchao Xuesheng Guanai Nongcun Jiaoyu—Hubei Jianlixian Guanai 'Kongchao Xuesheng'gongcheng Diaocha*" (Caring 'Students Left in Rural Areas' and Emphasising Rural Education—Investigation on 'Caring Students Left in Rural Areas' Program in Jianli County of Hubei Province)." *Tsinghua Journal of Education (Qinghua Daxue Jiaoyu Yanjiu)* (No. 2): 88–94.

Xiang, J. 2005. "*Nongmin Gong Zinu Jiaoyu: Zhengce Xuanze Yu Zhidu Baozhang – Guanyu Nongmin Gong Zinu Jiaoyu Wenti De Diaocha Fenxi Ji Zhengce Jianyi*" (the Education of Migrant Workers' Children: Policy Choice and Regulatory Guarantee – Analysis and Policy Recommendations for the Education of Migrant Workers' Children)." *Journal of Central China Normal University (Social Sciences)* (No. 3): 2–11.

Yang, N. 2009. "*Zhongguo quanmin jiaoyu fazhan de rogan wenti*" (A few issues in the development of education for all citizens in China). Speech given at the Seventh International Conference on Education Innovations, Hangzhou, China, 15–16 November. Accessed November 4, 2012. http://hxjy.com/v2templet/pg_interchange.asp?id=382&lm=%E5%AD%A6%E6%9C%AF%E9%A2%91%E9%81%93

Yinger, J. ed. 2004. *Helping Children Left Behind: State Aid and the Pursuit of Educational Equity.* Cambridge: MIT Press.

Zhou, Z., X. Sun, Y. Liu, and D. Zhou. 2005. "*Nongcun Liushou Ertong Xinli Fazhan Yu Jiaoyu Wenti*" (Psychological Development and Education Problems of Children Left in Rural Areas)." *Journal of Beijing Normal University in Social Sciences (Beijing Shifan Daxue Xuebao (Shehui Kexue Ban)* (No. 1): 71–78.

Index

For Product Safety Concerns and Information please contact our EU
representative GPSR@taylorandfrancis.com Taylor & Francis Verlag GmbH,
Kaufingerstraße 24, 80331 München, Germany

Printed and bound by CPI Group (UK) Ltd, Croydon, CR0 4YY

01/05/2025

01858353-0003